Alan Loach

Miles of Memories

A Solo Cycling Challenge Across Britain

For Rose – my angel in disguise

First published by Alan Loach 2024

Copyright © 2024 by Alan Loach

All rights reserved.

No part of this publication may be reproduced, distributed, or transmitted in any form or by any means, including photocopying, recording, or other electronic or mechanical methods, without the prior written permission of the author.

Book Cover by Alan Loach

The stories in this book reflect the author's recollection of events. Some names, locations, and identifying characteristics have been changed to protect the privacy of those depicted. Dialogue has been re-created from memory.

First edition

Contents

FORWORD 1

PREFACE 3

THE END IS THE BEGINNING 5

THE CHALLENGE - CAN I DO IT? 9

TODAY IS THE DAY - NO TURNING BACK 19

DAY ONE – THE END... ALREADY? 35

DAY TWO – NO BACON ROLLS.........................53

DAY THREE – FOLLOW THAT CAMEL...............63

DAY FOUR - THE ONLY WAY IS UP 79

DAY FIVE - A PLACE TO HIDEAWAY 93

DAY SIX - NEW AGE : NEW ROADS................105

DAY SEVEN - FOLLOW THE SEVERN..............115

DAY EIGHT - SCRAPES AND SCRAMBLES 127

DAY NINE - NETTLE BASHING........................139

DAY TEN - FINE DINING IN THE FOREST 151

DAY ELEVEN - THE HILLS... THE HILLS..........165

DAY TWELVE – PORRIDGE AND A LATTE 181

DAY THIRTEEN – ACROSS THE BORDER........195

DAY FOURTEEN – TAKE A BREAK 209

DAY FIFTEEN – BEAR NECESSITIES 221

DAY SIXTEEN - HEAD FOR THE HILLS 233

DAY SEVENTEEN - MIDGIE MAYHEM 245

DAY EIGHTEEN - DILEMMA IN DINGWALL............257

DAY NINETEEN - NC500 TO THURSO......................271

DAY TWENTY - HELLO JOHN O'GROATS 283

NEXT TIME - IF I DID IT AGAIN...............................295

SO WHEN ARE YOU GOING TO DO IT? 302

Forword

An introduction to Alan Loach, the author.

Alan Loach is a dedicated leisure cyclist who lives on the outskirts of Glasgow, is married, and has two adult children.

To his friends, Alan is a source of inspiration which can be attributed to the wealth of wisdom, knowledge, and the unique understanding that he brings to assist others while they encounter life, and life in all of its fullness. These attributes are grounded in his vibrant faith and his naturally positive outlook.

He is a qualified chef, has served as an IT specialist and advisor, and is an accomplished photographer who has also successfully graduated with honours at Art College – where one of his imaginative 3D sculptures depicting the streets of Glasgow won the end-of-year award.

Alan is an established explorer, both urban and rural, who is at home appreciating street architecture as well as navigating nature in the hills and glens – usually accompanied by his faithful travelling companion 'Chef Snoopy'.

A love for Scotland and its history has motivated an interest in the route travelled by St Mungo from Culross in Fife on the east coast, to Glasgow on the west coast, where St Mungo is recognised as the patron saint of this important Scottish city. The outcome of this research has resulted in a significant body of work which he is collating into his next literary project.

His current employment is as an administrator at a Community centre in the Queen's Park area where his organisation skills, his understanding of IT and his ability as a caring and compassionate supervisor have benefitted his fellow workers as well as those who use the very useful facilities this centre provides to the local community.

Alan is a man of passion, humility, and a great eye for detail – qualities that he incorporates into every aspect of his life and work, so sit back and enjoy Alan's adventure for its attention to detail, its important historic references, its local flavour and its delicious humour.

Stewart McCardle 2022

Alan Loach

Preface

So, what's this book all about then...

I had just finished my Land's End to John O'Groats cycle and people wanted to know about it:

'You must tell us all about your big cycle'

'You must have lots of stories about your trip'.

But I didn't. It was a familiar pattern. I would arrive home from work after a long day...

'What happened today at work, Alan?'. My mind goes blank. My brain lacks retention. The events of the day are filed in a hidden corner of my mind to make room for the next thing.

'I'll write it down', I thought, and as I did it all came back. Not only the journey, the places, the training, and planning, but stories of friends, family, other journeys, and memories from childhood.

So you don't need to be planning a cycle trip to read this book. It's a journey through my head as much as a journey across the country.

Join me and my co-rider Chef Snoopy, and we'll have some fun. You'll read about the highs and lows, and the literal ups and downs, find out some interesting facts about the places I cycled through, and eavesdrop on the conversations of the people I met.

If you're reading this book with the intent of cycling from Land's End to John O'Groats you'll be better prepared than I was from reading on.

Alan Loach 2023

Introduction

The End is the beginning

The midday August sun was beating down from the cloudless sky, and the heat haze distorted the ground in front of me. I sat motionless on my saddle, the wildflowers lining the gravel path ahead waved at me in the breeze, beckoning me to start my journey. I had been staring into the distance for ages, knowing I would need to get started. The blank look on my face probably caused people to stare and whisper.

'Do you think he's all right?'

The path ahead of me was 1200 miles long, much longer than the standard end-to-end route, and I tried to comprehend the distance. I had planned it all, but now I was actually standing here about to start my epic journey, I found it difficult to take in. I told myself it was just 120 one-hour cycles at 10mph to complete the whole journey. This sounded easier for some reason.

People milled about the coastal path enjoying the fine weather, eating ice cream, stopping for coffee, and capturing memories on their phones. Sensible people who came on buses, in cars, in motorhomes and on motorbikes. They would go back to the comfort of a bed for the night. I wouldn't see a proper bed for a while.

My co-rider Chef Snoopy was getting impatient. I needed to take that first step, or in my case the first turn of the pedals, but I was rooted to the spot. Why was I hesitating? Fear? No, I don't fear anymore. I would boldly go where many had been before. Panic? No, I'm not prone to panic. I'm a bit too chilled out for that. Anxiety? OK, I can get a bit anxious on occasion, but it doesn't last.

Why was I doing this? This is madness!

I wondered if the sunshine today and almost perfect cycling weather were giving me a false sense of security for the trip, I was prepared and not prepared, I knew what I faced ahead and at the same time didn't know. The known and the unknown swirled around my head. The scale of the journey was overwhelming me. I was about to embark on something I had planned in my head for what seemed like forever. I never thought I would have the chance to be standing here at Land's End ready to travel the roads and paths ahead of me that stretched the length of the whole country. I didn't want this moment to end, but I did need to get moving if I was going to get to John O'Groats.

Then reality kicked in, I *did* know why I was doing this. It was a deep personal need for challenge and adventure, but could I do it at my age? I imagined a giant holographic question mark hovering over the path I was about to take.

This was madness, but it was my madness!

I pushed down on my right pedal and my bike edged forward.

'This is it Snoop. Ready or not!'

Miles of Memories

The Challenge - Can I Do It?

'Alan!... Alan!...' Chef Snoopy, in his chef's hat, bright red apron and blue bow tie shouted at me from the bedside table, 'When are you going to do your Land's End to John O'Groats cycle?'

Odd, I thought, he doesn't speak in the cartoons.

'Time is running out!' he continued.

Suddenly I was fully awake, realising I'd been half asleep. Snoop sat on the bedside table where he always sat, just staring, silent, but his words rang in my ears. He was so annoyingly right sometimes.

'Well, I'm not doing it alone,' I told him. 'You'll need to come with me'.

That was the turning point.

Cycling from Land's End to John O'Groats (LEJOG) had been on my mind for a while, but the big question was, could I do it?

It was the unanswered question, and it had been a question for a long, long time, too long in fact. I was almost sixty years old and had done nothing about it.

Was it too late? Would I ever be fit enough to attempt it? Was I ever fit enough to do it in the first place?

Time, it would seem, passes faster as we get older, and those aspirations and ambitions we had when we were younger start to fade from our thoughts and memories. When they occasionally surface, we feel a sadness that we're probably too old now.

'If only I had...',

'I should have made more of an effort to...',

'It's too late now to...'

Sixty years old, was really old back in my younger days. People retired at sixty in those days. I remember watching The Sound of Music when I was about eight years old and seeing the young Von-Trapp romance developing.

'I am sixteen going on seventeen'. They sang and danced.

'That's really old' I thought to myself. In my naivety, I just couldn't imagine being that old.

And then there were my parents, in their forties when I was born and now heading for fifty. They seemed unbelievably old.

I mean, sixty years old at that time was when they retired you and sent you off to the scrapheap, didn't they? You would hobble along to the Post Office, bent over, and supported by your walking stick to pick up your pension on a Tuesday. These people would have croaky voices, and say things like:

'It's not the same as when I was young'

'The youngsters these days have no respect'.

Yet here I was, having reached that golden age when someone flips a switch and all of a sudden you're an OAP.

'Sixty is of course the new fifty', they now say.

Each milestone age has a phrase to make you feel a little better about yourself. But despite this, there is still a feeling that you're on a slippery slope, and to go with this comes a reminder of all the things you wanted to do in life but never quite got around to.

Cycling LEJOG was one of those things, a niggle in the back of my mind that kept returning over the years: the thought of doing it sparked in me a sense of adventure, a need to achieve, a fulfilment of something almost unattainable. It was the longest and most iconic A-to-B ride in the country. Thousands of cyclists completed it every year, and it had the appeal of being the ultimate

UK cycle. There were plenty of other planned routes in the UK, but LEJOG was the king of them all. The knowledge that you couldn't start a cycle any further south-west or finish any further north-east had a huge appeal.

Where do ideas come from? The sudden thought that pops into your head. The niggling feeling that you have to do something? Influences come from the world around us: advertising, conversations, news stories, and online. An accumulation of sources passing through our thought processes come together to set us off in a particular direction. But is this all purely chance, coincidence or some external influence? I guess it largely depends on what you believe. These days the Internet plays a big part. You do an innocent search for a cycling jacket and you're subsequently bombarded with ads for waterproof underpants, vests that glow in the dark, and the latest in cycle clothing 'technology' that you can't do without.

Faith played a big part in my life and decision-making, but did God want me to do LEJOG? Surely he had more important things to be concerned about in the world?...

All I knew was that the niggle had been there for a very long time and I would usually dismiss it as not really possible. The obstacles to doing it were many: getting the time off work; being able to afford the accommodation along the way and all the extra gear; being fit enough... I thought perhaps it was something I could do when I retired if I was still able and if the Government hadn't put up the state pension age yet again.

Another barrier was the image of the typical 'LEJOGer'. They would be a road cyclist, Lycra-clad, head-down cycling with others on main roads, have a backup vehicle, stay in B&Bs or bunkhouses, and complete the whole journey in seven to fourteen days. This wasn't me.

I was encouraged that the oldest person to complete LEJOG (at the time of writing) was a guy called Alex Menarry, who held the world record at 85 years old. He did it twice, the first time not logging it for the world record, so he did it again! An amazing achievement! He had support, and I wondered if there was a record for the oldest person who completed it totally self-supported, as I would be doing. However, I wasn't interested in beating any records. Just getting from one end to the other and surviving would be a good result.

I'd heard and read lots of stuff about LEJOG and the issues that could arise. Stories of people who had tried and given up – it was harder than they thought. I was told of someone getting pneumonia and being unable to continue, others had the weather against them and had a completely miserable time. Tales of experienced cyclists ending up under lorries, breaking limbs, and spending months in hospital. In hindsight, perhaps I shouldn't have Googled 'LEJOG Failures'.

I had done a couple of long-distance cycling trips a few years ago, but nothing like this distance, and on those trips, I had a proper bed every night.

This time I planned to camp. Could I cope with camping? I hadn't camped for over twenty years, and even then didn't really take to it. Would I have to abandon LEJOG after just a few days? After all, I was just a commuter cyclist, plodding my way to and from work at a very average pace.

Regardless of the doubts and potential barriers, I knew I just had to do LEJOG. My big SIX-OH birthday was approaching, and it would be a fitting challenge to do in my sixtieth year on this planet. A tick on my bucket list! I couldn't leave it any longer. However, I would need to do it as cost-effectively as possible, which meant camping and doing it alone.

This wouldn't be the first time I'd had a hare-brained idea. Fortunately, my wife, the sensible Mrs B, often brought me down to Earth, revealing the flaws in my thinking.

'Alan…. have you thought this through properly?'

And she was usually right, I hadn't, but thoughts and ideas would constantly flow through my head.

I asked other people who knew me what they thought of the LEJOG idea.

'So, you're thinking of doing it by yourself, with a tent and no support?'.

It was a pointed question. They obviously must have thought I was a bit mad by the tone of their voice.

'Erm yes, that's what I'll be doing' – raised eyebrows.

My ability or sanity was obviously in doubt, which was understandable. Some people would offer advice with concern, perhaps trying to put me off.

'It is of course a very long way, and many cyclists underestimate the effort required…'

I appreciated the concern, but I did intend to be as thorough as I could be with research and planning.

It would just be me and Chef Snoopy, no other support. We would be camping and carrying all our gear with us, we wouldn't be taking the easy option. True, we would be at the mercy of the elements and would have to cope with this ourselves, but I figured we would be a pretty resourceful team. Me, well I'd pushed through a few tough situations in life, and I knew I could do this!

So let me introduce my co-rider: Chef Snoopy. He took some convincing, but, after taking advice from Mr Shultz, a promise of root beer and pizza persuaded him to come along with me. Although I'm not confident about getting root beer in the UK, pizza wasn't going to be an issue. I would have cycled alone, a solitary time to gather my thoughts and consider the meaning of life, but I had known Chef Snoopy for a long time. He had been on many trips with Mrs B and myself and helped us out on several kids' camp cooking excursions in Aviemore. People said he was just a stuffed toy, but he was tough enough to shrug off insults like that. I was sure he was going to be a great help along the way.

So the planning and training began.

I started thinking about when. May in the UK was generally regarded as the driest month of the year, so I booked annual leave from work for the last week in April and the first two weeks in May (I'll explain later why I chose three weeks to do the cycle). However, the country went into COVID-19 lockdown just after Christmas 2020, and the prospect of much of the country being open in Spring 2021 was doubtful. So I changed my cycle dates to the last week in August and the first two weeks in September. The chances of good weather were mixed, but at least it shouldn't be too cold.

To do LEJOG in my sixtieth year I needed to do it before the Autumn of 2021, so this was my last chance before I turned 61.

The Autumn trip was a better decision on two fronts. April / May arrived and although some things were opening up after lockdown, the weather was bitterly cold for the time of year. Also in hindsight, I was nowhere near fit enough in April to tackle LEJOG, after a dip in my commuting distances over the winter.

The spring turned to summer and I upped my training days and mileage. I planned several days where I would go over the Campsie Fells north of Glasgow, climbing hills to over a thousand feet. I completed several sixty milers, some days more than this, and felt by the time August came that I was as ready as I would ever be to tackle LEJOG. (More on training later)

I tried to pack food with me on each training day that I might eat on my actual trip. I figured I could survive without the weight of a camping stove, pots and utensils and heating stuff up. On my training days, if I passed a

McDonald's, I would order via their app, asking it to be delivered to a collection point in the car park outside the restaurant – perfect! I did want to avoid eating out too much, one, to keep the cost of the trip down, and two, to save having to lock up my bike and trek into cafes with backpack, bags, and panniers in tow.

Little did I know that the reality of everything I had planned would be different on the actual trip.

Today is the day - No turning back

My alarm sprung to life at 4.30am. The day had come, this was happening. God willing I would be in Penzance by the end of the day! I still couldn't quite believe this fact. I was going over Plan B scenarios if things didn't work out.

Plan A was train number one to Glasgow - 15 minutes, train number two to Plymouth - 10 hours, then train number three to Penzance - 1.5 hours. My biggest concern was the train from Glasgow to Plymouth. Would my cycle booking be valid? The booking process was very odd. Would there be delays? After booking the train journey, I received an email from Cross Country Trains.

'Important upcoming engineering works'.

My heart sank. I was invited to visit their dedicated page to find out how it impacted my journey. A major junction was being upgraded near Birmingham and delays and diversions were planned. Fortunately, all the engineering works were occurring in the weeks before and the weeks after my journey, and there were no delays on my travel date! Yes!. But would this all go to plan? I had to be prepared for the unexpected. This was where Plan B sprang into action. This was a straightforward case of trying to catch a later train from Plymouth to Penzance. There were four other trains up to about 9pm.

Failing this Plan C would kick in if I was stuck in Plymouth for the night, where do I stay? I didn't research this much, but there were one or two campsites dotted around the area and I would be able to work this out once I arrived in Plymouth. So I wouldn't need to sleep on a park bench.

With everything pulled together, packed into my backpack, rack pack, panniers, front bag, and Chef Snoopy leading the way on the handlebars I left the house at 5.55am heading off to catch my first train. Mrs B waved me off.

'See you in two weeks!' I said, knowing I would be making a pit stop at home on the way to John O'Groats.

'Stay safe and come back in one piece!'. She prompted.

It was too late if I'd forgotten anything now! My first train was only a 15-minute journey, which got me into Glasgow far too early, but as booking the bike on this first leg wasn't possible, I didn't want to hit rush-hour commuters, full trains, and the possibility of being refused boarding with my bike.

I arrived at the historic Glasgow Central Station, built in the 1880s, and sat on the concourse scanning the boards for my train.

The 07.48 Cross Country train from Glasgow Central to Plymouth was on time, but I still pondered if I was going to get to Penzance today. Somehow it didn't seem real. The pending train journey itself was 10 hours. Faster options were available but included three or four changes. I didn't need the hassle of platform-hopping with a bike loaded with all my stuff, so after finding this direct service, with no changes, but lots of stops, all the way to Plymouth, I quickly booked it. Plymouth was as far as I could go in one journey.

The last hour and a half leg would be on a Great Western train to Penzance, and I had a 45-minute gap between the two services. I was hoping for no delays so I could make the connection.

The perennial issue for cyclists was getting their bikes on a train. A few times in the past I'd not been allowed to board a train as the cycle spaces were full. Fortunately, on both of today's booked journeys, I was able to book a cycle space, although booking a cycle space on the Cross Country service was a little odd. It wasn't possible to book a cycle space along with the train ticket, you had to send Cross Country a request through Facebook Messenger for a bike reservation! Really? I confirmed this by messaging Cross Country and was told by a nice chap called Nat that bike spaces were very limited.

'Best to request the bike space before booking the ticket' Nat advised.

As I waited in Glasgow Central, friends Stewart & Margaret appeared.

'We've come to see you off!'

It was great to see them and it took my mind off the doubts I was having.

A few weeks previously, Mrs B insisted that Chef Snoopy needed some waterproofs for this trip and had found some bright blue material for this. Margaret then sewed it together into a suitably sized waterproof jacket. With his trendy new waterproofs, Snoop was ready for anything.

Stewart worked for Scotrail until he retired but still had access to platforms and trains as an ex-employee. They saw me through the barriers, onto the train and helped me secure the bike in the bike storage area. 'Ready, Steady, Go!' Margaret took some photos as I left.

I had booked this train only six weeks previously. It wasn't possible to book seats sooner. The uncertainty of the Covid pandemic meant that train companies were a little cautious about taking bookings too far in advance. So I checked the Cross Country website a couple of times a day from the seven-weeks-to-go mark, and finally on the second of July bookings were open for my date. However, I happened to be on one of my training days when I checked, and halfway up the Campsie hills! Thankfully, I had a 4G data signal in the hills, and I was so glad it wasn't raining.

Remembering what Nat told me, I messaged Cross Country on Facebook Messenger to reserve the bike space hoping they would get back to me quickly.

I waited with some trepidation. Seating was still limited due to Covid restrictions and social distancing. Would the seat I wanted still be available by the time I went back to book the tickets? I paced up and down the country road I was on, nearby sheep were looking at me wondering what on Earth this human was doing next to their field, playing with his phone and muttering 'reply…. reply…. reply'

I waited fourteen tense minutes and was pinged a bike booking reference. I went back to the Cross Country website and booked the train there and then.

I'm quite up on tech, possibly because I worked in IT for 20 years, but I still find it amazing that you can do almost anything from anywhere now. I had just spent over a hundred pounds standing in the middle of nowhere with sheep as my only witnesses.

A huge sigh of relief came over me....

Then a little voice said,

'You booked the right day and time for the ticket and bike reservation didn't you?'.

I went back into the apps and checked – yes they matched! Phew! It seemed like a very odd system, so I messaged back asking if the bike booking and the train ticket could be linked. They couldn't –

'Different systems I'm afraid. When boarding the train, just show the guard your bike booking reference on Facebook Messenger'.

I moved on, elated that the biggest part of my journey had fallen into place.

I booked the Great Western 18.25 Plymouth to Penzance train later that day and my plans to get to Penzance were complete.

The train pulled up at Motherwell, and my good friend Jonathan joined me on his commute to work in

Edinburgh. Facemasks were still mandatory in Scotland on public transport, not so in England, so we chatted in a muffled kind of way, and with both of us being quietly spoken the conversation was interspersed with 'What was that?', 'Say that again?'. We chatted about the cycle and the challenge and the fact I had no support, and he wished me well for the journey, but I sensed him thinking

'You're a bit mad aren't you?'.

He was probably right.

When Jonathan got off at Edinburgh I sat alone for a while. The countryside flashed by with the occasional glimpse of the Forth estuary and the North Sea coast, as the train hurtled towards the English border.

As the train crossed into England, there was a simultaneous face mask removal by the surrounding passengers in the carriage. Mandatory masks had been lifted in England

I had with me a stock of John West Tuna Lunchpots, tins of baked beans and several Jordan's Frusli bars, so I popped a tuna pot for lunch. The idea was to stop along the way for food. These were backups, but on the train, lunch options were limited.

People came and went as I sat there, some people chatty some not, probably caught up in their own world. An elderly guy sat opposite me for a few stops, his first time outside his home since Covid struck, 18 months ago! – a changed world for him. Another lady poured out her woes of a son lost to a cult as she described it. I listened, empathised, and tried to make some encouraging noises.

I was reading a book for a while when another lady approached me with an accusation.

'You're in my seat!'

I looked up a little startled. She looked at me as if I'd committed a serious crime.

'I booked a window seat and you're in my seat'

I was in seat 48, a window seat. The seat next to me was 47, an aisle seat, and the seats on the other side of the table were 52 and 51.

I looked at Snoop, and he looked at me. His eyes were saying I should stand my ground.

'What's your seat number?' I asked. She ignored my question.

My ticket said 48A. I wasn't sure what the A was about as there was only one 48. I explained this to her, but she wasn't pleased.

An awkward silence.

'The window seat opposite is free - number 52' I suggested.

'We'll see what the conductor says when he comes round'. She sat diagonally opposite me in indignation.

If looks could have killed I wouldn't be writing this. What she didn't realise was that if she hadn't been so rude I would have just let her have my seat.

These kinds of situations used to worry me. Did I say something wrong? Did I look at her the wrong way? Should I just give in and give up my seat? I now realise that angry people often vent their anger not at the source of their anger, but at the first unfortunate soul who gets in the way. This seemed like one of those occasions; she was perhaps having a bad day. Yet despite trying to change the subject and engage her in conversation, which often works, she wasn't mellowing at all.

The conductor never arrived, and with a face like fizz, she got off the train after a few stops.

We approached Plymouth after 10 hours and I had about 45 minutes to wait for my connection. After finding the correct platform, I sat in the sunshine thankful that I'd made it this far. The connecting Great Western Railway train was on time and I boarded, secured my bike, and sat alone for the hour-and-a-half journey from Plymouth to Penzance.

On the train, I had plenty of time to review my route. I opened a book I had found a few months previously. It was a cycling guide published by Sustrans:

'Land's End to John O'Groats on the National Cycle Network'.

'on traffic-free paths and quiet roads' it promised. It sounded ideal, getting from one end of the country to the other without having to compete with other road users. The cover of the book presented an idyllic picture of a group of leisurely cyclists on a nice wide cycle path in some lovely countryside. The only drawback seemed to be that the meanderings to achieve this traffic freedom, stretched the route out to almost 1200 miles. I could cope with a few more miles I thought.

The book split the route into 28 stages, with distances ranging from 20 to 67 miles. So potentially four weeks if the cyclist took one stage per day.

'This is how I can do LEJOG', I thought.

Studying the book, I reckoned I could achieve sixty miles a day on moderately hilly sections, with perhaps twenty per cent less for very hilly sections and twenty per cent more for mostly flat sections. With the sixty miles a day average, and a total distance of just about 1200 miles, even though I didn't have enough fingers to count on, this worked out to 20 days. I would need three weeks off work. This seemed reasonable.

I plotted the Sustrans route in the cycling app Komoot and on an Excel spreadsheet. The spreadsheet was used to bring together all the info for each day, including the dates, timings, Komoot data, and campsites.

I reviewed these timings as the train headed westbound to my final destination, hoping my calculations were correct.

The train pushed through the countryside of the southwest, and I knew my cycling route would cross this train line in several places, so I kept a lookout for the locations where this would happen, taking a mental note of the surrounding countryside.

We pulled into Penzance, and I stepped off the train. The air was warm, humid, and salty.

'We made it Snoop – the adventure begins!' I could tell he was just as excited as I was, he just didn't show it.

The train station was close to the shore at the end of a promenade, which was dotted with tropical ferns and palm trees. Boats bobbed about in the harbour; it was like I'd stepped into the Mediterranean. I stood for a few moments to take it in, then realised that the evening was moving on and the sun was going down. I needed to get to the campsite.

A mile or so along the prom, past open-air cafés, and restaurants, I turned inland and uphill towards my first campsite which was on the outskirts of the town. With Penzance being a fairly small town, I was there in no time.

I was booked in at the YHA Penzance, camping in the grounds of the main house, Castle Horneck Lodge, an old Georgian mansion set in a few acres and surrounded by wooded gardens. The lodge was a big house with bookable rooms as well as a campsite.

The friendly girl at reception confirmed breakfast times and the layout of the site. Several large, fixed tents occupied a small field next to the lodge, and a general camping site was located further away after trekking along a short path through a few trees to a larger unlit field behind the lodge. I was going to need my head torch when it got dark.

It was 8.30pm as I pitched my tent for the first night, relieved to be able to catch the last of the light to get the tent up. This was only my second time pitching this tent.

The first tent pitch was in my back garden before I left home, where I spent a few nights getting used to sleeping out in it. I hadn't camped for about 20 years and even then, wasn't a seasoned camper. But the nights in the back garden were good practice for LEJOG.

I hardly slept that first night at home in the garden. Every outdoor noise seemed to be magnified. The house was within earshot of a motorway and subject to the constant drone of traffic which persisted even through the night. And then the noise of the wildlife; owls and other assorted birds were incredibly noisy!

After a couple of nights however, the noises seemed to fade. My brain was tuning them out, much like when shop workers tune out the in-store music as it repeats throughout the day as they work.

Only one other small tent was pitched in the YHA camping field, and the site was not near any main roads, so I was hoping for a quiet night.

By the time I had blown up my ground mat and pillow and unfolded my sleeping bag, the waves of tiredness caught up with me. It had been a very long day, 17 hours and six hundred miles from waking in the morning to now, I was exhausted. I hadn't eaten much, so ate a second John West Tuna Lunch Pot and a chocolate bar.

'Snoop, I can't believe we're here!'

I couldn't believe it. This was a dream, a huge ambition. Was this happening? Was I really in Penzance, only 15 miles from Land's End? I lay in my sleeping bag staring at the tent around me. The route for the next day ran through my head. I had travelled the route on Google Streetview and had seen where I was going to cycle on a computer screen. Tomorrow, I would cycle it for real.

After calling Mrs B to let her know I'd arrived safely, I settled down for the night and drifted off into a peaceful sleep.

It was a quiet night, but I had to trek to the toilet three times. The toilet block with washing facilities and showers was a building next to the main house. I was so thankful for the head torch that Mrs B had bought me. In the pitch-black, it was a matter of crossing the field, through the woods and into the floodlit toilet block. By the time I got back, I was wide awake!

Mrs B looked after me so well and knew me better than I knew myself.

'Alan, I've bought you a head torch for your cycle, you might need it.', she handed me a strap with a light on it. I looked at it suspiciously.

'I'm not sure I'll need a head torch really', my stubborn response, thinking, 'Why does she waste money on things I don't need?'

'Trust me and just take it anyway', she said not backing down. As persistent as ever.

'OK if you insist.' Not really wanting to.

I needed it.

She was right.

When will I learn?

Miles of Memories

Day one – The End... already?

Good morning, Penzance!

I hadn't slept much, a mixture of excitement and the new surroundings. But I was awake and eager to start the day.

Chef Snoopy was already awake. I think he'd been awake all night.

'Well Snoop?', I asked, 'Where's my coffee?'

He just stared back at me.

'Only joking Snoop!' we didn't have a camping stove to heat water for coffee anyway. He wasn't laughing.

At the time of booking the YHA tent pitch for my two nights here, I also booked a full breakfast for each morning, so I unzipped the tent to make my way to the house.

The morning was bright and warm, cloudy with bursts of sunshine. Trekking through the woods to the main house, the air was fresh and scented with wildflowers.

'Good morning!', the cheery man behind the breakfast bar smiled and asked me what I would like.

'The whole works please'

I had bacon, fried eggs, sausage, hash brown, baked beans, and tomato. This was accompanied by a latte, and I felt set up to tackle the day. I thought with a Cornish Breakfast I might be offered a Cornish Pasty, but no, not a Cornish pasty in sight.

'We're in Cornwall Snoop' as if he didn't know, 'we must get a real Cornish Pasty'.

A few other campers came in for breakfast. Some took it back to their tents. A great arrangement, camping and breakfast made for you. Other facilities included a café, bar, laundry, drying room, games room and a BBQ area. Hardly roughing it, this was camping with style!

My plan for today was to cycle 15 miles to Land's End and 15 miles back, returning to the YHA campsite. So, two nights camping in Penzance. Therefore, there was no rush to get away early this morning, as I had the whole day to cover just 30 miles.

I considered cycling a longer round trip to Land's End rather than cycling there and back on the same route, but at the last minute decided to stick to my plan to do the trip on the National Cycle Network route 3 (NCN3) there and back and spend more time at Land's End and in Penzance.

Breakfast finished and I was thankful that I could leave the tent pitched and carry a lesser load to Land's End.

I set up Komoot as my satnav on an old phone attached to my top bar and also started Strava running to record the route on my main phone.

At home, I would track my commutes and training days in the app Strava, a cycle-tracking app for those who don't know. It captures your stats: mph, distance, time, and heart rate if linked to a monitor, and has the potential for a whole lot more. It compels you to be quite competitive, highlighting your best time for specific sections of the road, and if you cycle a certain segment more times than anyone else in a certain period of time, then you become a 'Local Legend'. On top of this, there's a leaderboard for those who have completed segments in the fastest time. Needless to say, I was way down the leaderboard with my leisurely commutes. I was happy just to use it to record my mileage over the week or month, so I knew how far the bike had gone over its lifetime (in the absence of a bike odometer - another gadget). Having said this, it was useful in training to measure progress and know my limitations for a big cycle.

I set off from the campsite in the sunshine, with Chef Snoopy riding on the handlebars, and headed for the Penzance promenade.

Penzance seemed like a very pleasant place. Not overly touristy, with some nice shops and cafes, and retaining elements of its fishing heritage and legendary pirates.

I headed west, feeling that this was a perfect day for the journey to Land's End, the wind was light, the air fresh with a hint of saltiness, and the dappled sunshine drifted in the direction of Land's End willing me on.

'We're off Snoop. Let's go!!'

The route led me past Newlyn, a lively harbour, and the hub of the local fishing trade as well as for pleasure craft. A queue had formed outside the harbour fish shop, Trelawney Fish & Deli, where presumably the catch of the day was available for purchase. The 'Today's Specials' board displayed a couple of dozen varieties of fish & shellfish. If I had somewhere to cook food I might have stopped and bought something on my return journey.

Following the coast road, I arrived at the charming village of Mousehole, locally known as Mousel, once part of a busy local pilchard industry. It's narrow streets and tiny cottages, gathered around a harbour filled with small wooden fishing boats. Now a holiday destination with nice gift shops and cafes.

Mousehole was charming until the road out of the village headed uphill for half a mile at a very steep incline - its charm faded fast. My first taste of the infamous Cornish hills.

'Well Snoop, do you think we can make it up that hill?'

He just stared ahead at the impossible gradient and didn't say a word. But I knew what he was thinking – he didn't care as he wasn't pedalling. Fair enough I thought.

I tried my very best, quite determined to get to the top without stopping, getting off and pushing the bike, but I failed halfway up. I got off and pushed.

'So, you've not even got to the start of your LEJOG yet and you're pushing the bike up hills already,' I thought to myself.

It would be the first time of many times. Even when crossing the Pennines ten years earlier, as the road rose to over two thousand feet, did I get off and push then? No. I'd barely gone five miles in Cornwall and had been beaten by a tiny Cornish fishing village. Snoop respected my shame by staying silent.

Relieved to get to the top of the hill, the quaint, narrow country lanes and rich fertile landscape led me on from here on gentler inclines and I arrived at St Buryan, just over halfway to my destination. Time for a break, I purchased bananas from a local shop, sat on a rustic-looking bench by a bus stop and watched as the Land's End Coaster open-top bus sailed by with camera-snapping Japanese tourists hanging over the top deck.

'Morning!' I shouted, giving them a wave with banana in hand.

The cameras turned in my direction and I had visions of my image whizzing across the globe to appear on Japanese social media.

クレイジーバナナマン
(Crazy banana man!)

Setting off again I was looking forward to getting to Land's End to start my end-to-end trek in earnest. More country lanes, and then a view of the sea. I was close. Sennan Cove and Whitesand Bay came into view. The idyllic-looking beach was busy, and surfers rode the waves offshore. A car park above the cove was jam-packed with cars, their occupants walking down the hill to the lovely sandy beach to do what people do on a beach in the sunshine. The August Bank Holiday was approaching, and in England, it was still the school holidays, so it was no surprise that the place was busy.

My route didn't go down the hill too far, but halfway down headed off on a level road parallel to the shore. I was quite relieved at this, as I was quickly learning that steep downhills are often followed by steep uphills.

Shortly Land's End came into view. I cycled towards the car park, following a car. Cars pay £7 for the privilege of parking here.

'Is there a charge for bikes?' I asked passing the pay kiosk.

'No, carry on.'

I guess it wouldn't be enforceable for bikes with the many paths leading here, so I knew the answer I would get. I just wanted the simple pleasure of being told I didn't have to pay!

Land's End was rather touristy, and I wasn't interested in what the 'Land's End Attraction' had to offer. The grand entrance to this stood at the end of the incoming road. Visitors could park their cars and explore the white-washed buildings beyond the entrance archways and columns to find shops, arcades, and a host of other places to spend their hard-earned cash.

I headed around the outside of the buildings to arrive at the rugged coastline.

The weather at Land's End was perfect. Sunshine and a gentle breeze. Along the coastline, the gentle rollers lapped the rocks below the viewing points, and birds circled and dived just off the shore. Gannets, fulmars, kittiwakes, shags, razorbills, and the Cornish chough, could be seen here. There were certainly plenty of gulls making a play for visitors' unattended food, not helped by people throwing chips to them, and the subsequent scrabble of birds.

Rugged vegetation clung to the rocks. Wildflowers such as thrift, sea campion and wild thyme carpeted the cliff tops. I overheard a local guide saying that if you're lucky, you might catch sight of grey seals, basking sharks and dolphins in the waters below.

I could tell that Chef Snoopy was impressed. Trying to spot a glimpse of the sea life, he silently stared out to sea for ages.

The Southwest Coastal Path passed through here, the north section meeting the south section. 500 miles of path from Minehead to Poole, making it the longest continuous footpath in the country. The promise of spectacular cliff-top walks was very appealing, but this would need to wait until another time.

The famous signpost was there for all to see. Unfortunately, a photo opportunity by the post was going to cost me, the area had been cordoned off by a professional photography outfit, and it wasn't possible to get close to it to take your own photos. Although I imagine if you got here early enough to start your LEJOG before the photographers arrived, then you might stand a chance of snapping your own photo.

It was about midday, and a long queue of people waited in turn to get their official photos. Part of the service was that they would put the name of your hometown, and the distance to it, on a finger of the signpost, then take your picture. This would be your 'Personalised Souvenir Photo from Land's End', all at prices starting from £10.80 for one 7 x 5-inch print. I didn't bother and took a bunch of selfies instead. Although the queue of people obscured the signpost, and I couldn't get a decent selfie shot with the post.

The place was buzzing with people, but seeing through all this I liked Land's End itself, and if I didn't have the bike and had more time, I would have been getting away from the crowds, scrambling over the rocks, cliffs and headlands. I decided a revisit with Mrs B would be on the cards someday.

I had started a travel tracker app on my phone in Glasgow as I set off on my journey. The app Polarsteps had been tracking my progress so far. In hindsight, it would have been better to start it here at Land's End – a cleaner A-to-B tracked route. As it was, it tracked my whole train journey, so the total miles when I got to the end wouldn't be representative of the actual LEJOG cycle. Like many things, there was a learning curve.

Polarsteps itself was proving great for this kind of trip. People could follow you via the app or on the Internet and could see where you were in real-time. A moving dot on the map. And the app allowed the traveller to add photos and text at any point along the way. I was posting each Polarsteps blog entry to Facebook also and was surprised by how many people were connecting with it. My routine with the blog turned into posting a few times a day and summarising the day before my head hit the pillow at night.

So, this was it, the start of my journey. I paused for a while to reflect on the challenge ahead, fleeting moments of doubt as I imagined the journey ahead. I was going to attempt to cycle the whole length of the country. Oh my, was I up for this?

But with a realisation that I had almost 1200 miles to go, I set off without an ounce of trepidation or foreboding.

My concerns had evaporated, but was this a false sense of confidence because of today's good weather and the easy first cycle? Would I make it all the way?

'John O'Groats here we come! Ready or not!'. Snoop was as excited as I was.

Heading back to Penzance the August afternoon sun was high in the sky, and the quiet winding back roads of NCN3 made the cycle back a joy. The countryside looked very different cycling in the opposite direction. This was the windswept Penwith peninsular, which was the hook of land at the tip of Cornwall, once its own local government district.

As I cycled back through the narrow roads and high hedges that characterised Cornwall, a bus appeared and took up the whole width of the road. It was another Land's End open-top bus, like the one I had seen earlier in St Buryan.

These buses do a complete circuit of the peninsular, one going clockwise and the other anticlockwise. The whole three-and-a-half-hour journey takes in most of the attractions around the coast including St Ives, St Just and Cape Cornwall, Pendeer Tin Mine, Land's End, and the Minack Theatre. Travellers could buy a day or weekly ticket for the buses and hop on and off at their leisure.

There was no way I could cycle past this bus as it took up the whole width of the road, so I had to pull into the side in a gap in the hedge and it sailed by, the driver giving me a friendly wave. I was just thankful I wasn't in a car for this encounter.

I was looking forward to the cycle downhill into Mousehole, but to get there involved going uphill at Lamorna, another get-off-and-push episode. In hindsight, I should have looked at the route profile in my Kamoot app and found a route with a gentler incline, if there was such a route. This would be a recurring theme as the days went on.

Mid-afternoon I arrived back in Penzance looking for a latte to celebrate the start of my end-to-end trek. Warren's Bakery in the main shopping street looked like a good choice.

'The Oldest Cornish Pasty Maker in the World' it said on the sign. I imagined some really old guy in the back of the shop making pasties, but then realised it was the bakery and not the baker that was old! Never having had a genuine Cornish Pasty from Cornwall, largely because I'd never been to Cornwall before, I wondered if I should have one now, at 4pm, or have fish & chips. The occasional smell of fish & chips from an unseen chip shop wafted through the air, and it won the day. 'I'll get a Cornish Pasty tomorrow', I promised myself. Cornish Pasty failure number one.

I wandered around Penzance, checking the place out for a possible return with Mrs B. There were narrow streets with cobbles, old fishermen's houses, and some lovely areas such as the promenade and gardens with sub-tropical plants. There was also an eclectic range of people on the streets, from retirees and holidaymakers to well-off and not-so-well-off locals.

I said hello to some people in passing and a couple of times hadn't a clue what they said in response. It sounded friendly and I figured it must be the Cornish dialect or language.

These are some of the Cornish greetings.

Dydh da	Hello
Fatla genes?	How's it going with you?
Fatel os ta?	How are you?

I didn't try any of these!

First-time visitors to some parts of Scotland face a similar dilemma. Having arrived in Scotland as a shy twelve-year-old English boy I can testify to this.

'Whir d'ya cum freae?' was a common question when I started school. It wasn't easy, but my ear eventually tuned to the dialect, and I told them 'where I came from', which caused much hilarity with my Lancashire accent.

'Can yeh say: 'It's a braw bricht moonlicht nicht the nicht'

I can't remember if I did actually try and say this, but I became a source of much entertainment for my peers.

I spotted references to pirates as I walked through Penzance, which also brought back memories of my school days and Gilbert and Sullivan's comic opera, The Pirates of Penzance.

At the end of every school year, our school would put on a play and for several years, they chose Gilbert and Sullivan operas. The ensemble comprised of senior pupils in their final years at school, who were chosen while spending their free periods in the music class. This included me this year; I was one of the pirate ensemble. How on Earth I got a part singing in a chorus I'll never know; they must have been desperate. Mrs B can testify that I can't actually sing a note in tune. But in that class I was, and they chose me, along with most of the class, to be honest, picked, I guess, to boost the pirate hoard.

The music teacher picked out baritones and tenors from the motley crew in front of him. I was put in the group of tenors and struggled a bit with the higher notes. I thought at the time that perhaps I should have been a baritone, not knowing if my voice had broken or not, but now I realise that the issue was that I just couldn't sing at all.

We all had pirate costumes, were plastered in stage makeup, and carried wooden swords fashioned by the art department to match our wooden acting skills.

At one point in rehearsals, I had a bright idea. I brought to school a real sword from home (doesn't every home have one?) and the music teacher nearly had a heart attack. I was told in no uncertain terms that it was not allowed. (I was incredibly naive). The sword was blunt, what's the problem?

To clarify the sword thing, at the time my parents owned a hotel; a really old castle-type hotel, and we had swords on the wall. I just borrowed one on the way to school one day, as any schoolboy would... All I can say is that it's a good thing I was a pretty docile child. I'd been bullied at school and could have easily reaped my revenge with that sword.

In Penzance, I found my fish & chips at the appropriately named Pirate's Rest just off the seafront and it was truly delicious. Fresh fish from Newlyn Harbour half a mile away! I sat on a bench on the promenade to eat, looking out to sea, watching the boats gently bobbing around in the bay. Mrs B would love it here.

Back in the tent, I looked at my route for day two in the Komoot app. The Komoot elevation profile showed the rise and fall of the hills as colour-keyed sections. Green for flat and shallow inclines, orange for moderately steep inclines and red for very steep inclines. The steep hills I encountered today were in the red zone. I made a mental note to pay more attention to this on subsequent days.

Day two had several orange sections, so I knew I had a few hills to climb, but I assumed that if they weren't red then they were probably manageable. The chosen route stuck to NCN3 and I figured deviating from this too much at this point was stepping into the unknown at this late stage. Also, it wasn't easy to modify a route in the Kamoot app on my phone. It was much easier to modify routes on a PC on the Komoot website. So, I just decided to run with what I'd planned.

In the camping field, the previous night's campers had left, and another party of campers arrived – a bunch of youngsters with a big tent and an awning with a table and chairs. I thought I'd say hello.

'Hi, you on holiday?' What else would they be doing here? But debatably a better question than 'Nice weather, isn't it?...' - an ice breaker, nonetheless.

'Visiting friends in Penzance', one of the girls replied

'Great! Amazing weather for camping'. Had to mention the weather after all, and it was a conversation stopper.

'Yeh...'

They didn't ask what I was doing, so I thought I would tell them anyway.

'I'm cycling to John O'Groats. Heading east tomorrow for my first big cycle', I said expecting at least a raised eyebrow, but my revelation drew blank looks. Perhaps they just weren't interested, or more likely they had no clue where John O'Groats was. Anyway, I sensed trouble.

I settled down for the night, called Mrs B, and then nodded off. Hopefully, I would sleep a bit better tonight. I had fifty-five miles to cover tomorrow and a few more Cornish hills.

I awoke with a start at 11pm. The young campers arrived back at the campsite, after a night out, laughing out loud, their voices boomed around the campsite presumably boosted in volume by the alcohol. They then sat up chatting and joking until the early hours.

They must have missed the sign asking campers to be respectfully quiet after 10pm. I pulled the sleeping bag over my head, but it didn't make much difference.

Day two – No Bacon Rolls

I woke at 6am just as it started to get light, I hadn't slept much with the noise in the early hours. Zipping open the tent, everything was covered in dew, and a mist had descended over the campsite. But there was no rain and it was sixteen degrees even at this time in the morning.

Today's cycle would see me heading east for a few miles, crossing the Penwith peninsular and skimming the north Cornish coast before heading through Truro, Cornwall's capital, and then heading back to the north coast at Newquay. The final leg then heading inland to a campsite at Ruthvoes.

Breakfast was a repeat of yesterday, and probably more needed today to sustain me over the fifty-five miles of ups and downs! Today was the day when the serious cycling began. As I demolished my breakfast, a guy at the next table noticed from my dress sense that I must be on a cycling trip.

'Where are you heading?'. It was a question I would hear many times over the next three weeks.

'John O'Groats – eventually'

'I'm so envious. I really would like to do that, but with my responsibilities, it's just not possible – I have a young family'

The perennial problem. We make choices in life and fill our lives with so many things that we don't leave time to fit in the things in life that truly fulfil us.

'My family are grown up now. Your time will come when they're older. Maybe your son would do it with you?'

He asked for the link to my blog,

'It might give me some ideas of how I can do it.'

'Anything I can do to help!' I emailed him the link.

Breakfast finished and I headed back to the camping field, packed up the tent after shaking the dew off it as noisily as I could, and set off down the hill to the promenade. The mist was still low. I thought about the Cornish pasty I had promised myself the day before, but at just before 8am Warren's Bakers hadn't opened yet!

'Didn't think that one through very well did you, Alan'. Cornish Pasty fail number two. I could sense Chef Snoopy sniggering in silent insolence. He had no respect sometimes.

I picked up NCN3 again, this time heading east along the south coast. The route skirted the shore for a few miles along the Southwest Coastal Path. The sea was calm but ebbed and flowed on the sand of Long Rock beach with a calming rhythmic sound.

Hidden in the mist across the water of Mounts Bay was the tidal island of St Michael's Mount, a rocky island which held a twelfth-century castle and medieval church. Now in the care of the National Trust. Visitors could visit the island at low tide via a causeway.

NCN3 quickly turned inland to cross the narrow peninsular to Hayle on the Cornish north coast where the weather brightened.

In its heyday, Hayle was a foundry town and port, famed for its smelting of copper and the invention and production of Cornish engines and boilers.

When planning my cycle, I found a recommendation for Philps Bakery in Hayle and intended to stop for one of their 'award-winning' Cornish Pasties. But I was so driven to make progress I completely forgot to stop. In fact, I cycled right past the shop despite PHILPS being plastered in large lettering on the building in several places. In my defence, I was cycling a main road through the town at the time with traffic on my tail, so may have been concentrating on not getting flattened by a car. Cornish Pasty failure number three.

'Not a word Snoop....' I said (Not that he ever really spoke anyway)

The path out of Hayle headed east and into a light easterly breeze. I had hoped, as many LEJOGers do, for a south-westerly prevailing wind to help me along my way. This was the norm at this time of the year, but the east wind wasn't strong at all. However, the wind can have a surprisingly big influence on timings when cycling, and I've often said in the past that I would prefer to cycle in the rain than cycle into a headwind. So, I was aware that the easterly breeze, despite being light, may take the edge off my timings.

Passing by the Estuary and Copperhouse Creek RSPB reserves, but not having time to stop for long and birdwatch, I discovered from an info board that the tidal estuary water here never freezes as it's so far south and as coastal as you can get. The mild conditions provided a haven for Curlew, Little Egret, Oyster Catchers, and Widgeon.

The route then headed uphill past whitewashed Cornish cottages and onto country roads with the hedges getting higher and higher as the road progressed. Cornish villages with narrow streets appeared every few miles along the way and the hedges started meeting overhead creating tunnels of trees.

I arrived in Camborne, known in the late eighteenth and early nineteenth centuries as the centre of the Cornish tin and copper mining industry. Today visitors are encouraged to follow its heritage trail to discover the achievements of the town such as Richard Trevithick's 'Puffing Devil', a steam carriage that gave rise to trains and cars. Or visit the remaining buildings of the Camborne School of Mines, where Cornish miners honed their skills, and subsequently carried them all over the world.

I cycled past Trevithick's statue in Camborne and saw a signpost to Troon. I was immediately transported to Troon on the Ayrshire coast - in my head that is. (At the time of writing Star Trek style transporting hadn't been invented). Sand dunes, ice cream on the seafront and fish & chips at the harbour. This wasn't the same Troon, but I could almost smell and taste the salt & vinegar. I realised I was hungry.

The landscape was dotted with the chimney stacks of old mines which once produced copper ore, black tin, and pyrite.

Redruth, once one of the largest and richest mining areas in Britain, came and went and the hills were getting steeper. Despite Kamoot saying they were 'orange' hills, they must have been very close to the red zone. A hill just after Redruth was particularly steep, and yes, I was out of the saddle and pushing the bike again.

I was pleased to make it to Truro in what seemed like a good time. Just over halfway.

Dominating the city, the three-spired Truro Cathedral, built between 1880 and 1910, was one of the most iconic buildings in Cornwall, with over 200,000 visitors a year. I would have loved to have had time to stop and explore.

I sat in the Truro town centre pedestrian area amongst the familiar sight of high street shops, purchased a latte from Café Nero and inadvertently fell into Cornish Pasty fail number four. I could have had one for lunch, but the thought went completely out of my head. I opened a tin of beans.

'Nice place Snoop,' I said as Chef Snoopy sat next to me on a city centre bench. He was people-watching. I could tell.

My daily plan seemed to be working OK so far. I had been following a plan which I worked out in training. It went like this: I would cycle for one hour, then take a 10 to 15-minute break. This would repeat until lunchtime when I would take a one-hour break. This would give time for lunch, snacks, photo stops and toilet stops.

In Truro, however, I was getting a little restless after 45 minutes, so I headed off, cycling another hour, and again taking 10 to 15-minute breaks until my destination.

By the time I reached Newquay, nine miles from the campsite, my backside was making itself known and I was starving. I spotted a McDonald's on the edge of town and pulled in. I ordered the largest burger meal they had, a Big Tasty with bacon, plus fries, plus an Oasis drink. It was totally delicious, but in hindsight, this probably didn't do me much good as I felt bloated and lethargic afterwards.

The cycle route skimmed Newquay, so I didn't see much of the town itself, and I pretty much dragged my bike and body those last few miles to the campsite just outside the small village of Ruthvoes.

The campsite entrance with its sign stating 'Piggies Camping' was a very welcome sight.

'Do you think pigs are camping here Snoop?'. He gave me a look out of the corner of his eye. He wasn't amused.

It was 6pm, I had cycled only fifty-five miles and was exhausted and saddle sore, totally drained. Not only that, but the day's cycle also had taken me an hour and a half longer than I planned. This was concerning as tomorrow was longer in miles and higher in elevation.

Piggies campsite was very well kept, the grassed areas lovely and flat and freshly mown. A sign at the entrance gave two mobile numbers for the owners of the site – 'call us when you arrive' it said. I called one of the numbers, explaining I had booked a pitch and had just arrived. A man appeared from a nearby caravan.

'Hello, my name is Alan' I prompted.

'Ah yes, glad you made it'. I guess he must have seen my look of exhaustion.

I explained that I would be simply pitching my tent and leaving quite early in the morning.

'Well, our rate is £16 a night, but we'll just call it a tenner'. I handed over a tenner, thanking him for his generosity.

'Not a problem. We get a few cyclists heading through here for John O'Groats, and the costs can mount up over the whole journey'. He gave me a nice quiet corner opposite a couple of camper vans with awnings.

As I set up the tent, a lady from one of the vans was cooking dinner for her family outside on a camping stove.

'I would love to do Land's End to John O'Groats,' she said. She was probably in her forties

'I cycle and run, in fact, I'm a bit of a fitness freak.' Her teenage daughter rolled her eyes as if saying here she goes again! I explained I was more or less following the National Cycle Network for much of the journey and flashed the Sustrans book. At this point, I wasn't doubting my choice of route as much as I would do later.

'If you want a cup of tea later let me know,' she said. I thanked her but I just wanted to sleep. I crawled into my tent and lay there completely still in exhaustion.

I was surprised that I was so tired. I was never this tired after my training days when I'd gone much further than 55 miles. Perhaps it was the headwind? The planned Komoot route told me the elevation for today's hills was 3500ft which I'd also done in training, but it felt like much more than this. I also had the app Strava running and it clocked the actual ascents at 4680ft! No wonder I was tired. I had cycled up the equivalent height of the UK's highest mountain: Ben Nevis, and then some!

I called Mrs B to offload my woes.

'I'm struggling, and it's only day two, and only day one of the sixty milers...'

She listened to my grumbles, heard about the aches, and sympathised with my tiredness.

'Keep going, I'm praying for you.'

I probably wasn't making much sense as I was so tired. I hung up and was soon sleeping. I dreamed of bacon rolls with wings flying over the Cornish landscape and landing softly on the grass.

Day three – Follow That Camel

I woke early, about 5.30, eager to make a start and push on to get to my next campsite in good time. With yesterday's cycle taking much longer than planned I was a little concerned about today, which was five miles further and a few hundred feet higher – according to the Komoot app, which appeared to let me down yesterday. But which was more accurate, Komoot or Strava? I decided that I perhaps needed to rely less on technology and just go for it. I would still run Komoot as it was my satnav, keeping me on my route, but to conserve battery power I wouldn't use Strava.

After speaking to Mrs B the night before about my worries and woes, she'd started sending me encouraging texts.

'You can do this! …'

Yes, I could do it. I was going to do it!

'We need a bacon roll Snoop'. I recalled my dream, and I was hungry. The site was called Piggies, but not a pig in sight. The owner said that people do expect it to be a pig farm, and they've even had to state on their website that there are no pigs onsite.

'Ah well Snoop, we'll just need to get breakfast somewhere else' Chef Snoopy looked as disappointed as I was, and there was no consoling him.

With renewed enthusiasm we were back on the road by 7.30am to get a head start, this was to become a recurring theme.

I initially would be travelling north today to Padstow, before looping around to Bodmin and then fixing on a northeast trajectory parallel to the Cornish north coast. My destination was a campsite near Holsworthy.

I left Piggies to retrace my steps back to the cycle route, which meant a couple of miles back the way I came to pick up NCN3 and make my way through to the town of St Columb Major. However, there was a quicker way to Saint Columb Major which was half the distance but along a potentially busier road. This was an easy diversion and didn't involve any major rerouting, but it was a bit of a gamble not knowing the local roads. Would the road be busy with bleary-eyed rush-hour commuters? Then I remembered it was Saturday, so perhaps less morning traffic than mid-week? I decided to go for it and took the shorter option. As it turned out there was hardly a car on the road, and I cut a couple of miles off my route.

I cycled through Saint Columb Major, a town with extremely narrow streets, and bags of history, but not a bacon roll in sight. I guess it was only 7.45am.

I discovered that here a medieval game called Hurling was played twice a year, where two teams of locals: the Townsmen (from St Columb town) and the Countrymen (from the rest of the parish) would carry a silver ball to goals set two miles apart. The whole town seemed to get involved and from the sound of it, there was quite a festival air to the proceedings. It sounded like a slightly strange version of Rugby. I spotted a pub named after the sport, 'The Silver Ball', on the way through.

The route beyond St Columb Major took me through lots of narrow country roads, through the small village of Rumford, still no bacon rolls, until I reached Padstow. Tesco appeared on the way into Padstow. I pulled in, thinking most bigger Tesco stores have a café, and possibly bacon rolls... No café.

Continuing down the hill into Padstow my route swung east, missing the town centre and harbour, heading to the cycle route along the River Camel.

Surely a riverside café would be open for breakfast. It was just after 8.30am, and nothing was open. I could have headed back into the town centre, but I knew that time was precious after my longer-than-expected trek yesterday, and I needed to push on. We had quite a few miles ahead on the Camel Trail before we would come to any more cafes.

'Well Snoop, I don't think we're getting a bacon roll'

I could see that look of desperation in his eyes, I knew how he felt.

Looking back at the map later I would realise that Padstow was a huge diversion that was probably unnecessary. St Columb Major to Bodmin was twelve miles direct, avoiding busy roads, but via Padstow, it was twenty-two miles, all for the sake of sticking to the National Cycle Network. Ah, the benefits of hindsight!

From Padstow, the route followed the Camel Trail, an 18-mile cycle path that ran parallel to the River Camel along a disused railway line from Padstow to Wenfordbridge via Bodmin.

The name 'Camel' was nothing to do with the humped variety found in dryer regions of the world, but came from the Cornish name 'Dowr Kammel', which meant crooked river.

Chef Snoopy had never seen a camel so got very excited in his inanimate way.

'There won't be any camels, it's just the name of the river' I told him. Not sure he believed me.

The original Bodmin to Wadebridge Railway opened in 1834 to transport sand to the farms on Bodmin Moor to help improve the soil quality. So being a railway, the route was quite flat, however, the surface was gritty and not as smooth as a road. Not conducive to turning up the pace to get to where you needed to go. The break from the hills was however welcome, and a steady pace was possible.

Many disused railways up and down the country had been transformed into cycleways, opening up the countryside to budding off-the-road cyclists and walkers. These routes were great for the casual cyclist and the going was generally easy. The Camel Trail ticked all the boxes for leisurely day-out-on-the-bike cyclists, river views, trees gracefully arching over the path, stopping places with picnic benches, and railway history dotted along the trail.

For those on a mission, which is cycling from one end of the country to the other, the focus on getting there overshadowed the more leisurely aspects of the route.

Having said that, one of my favourite parts of cycling a disused rail line is seeing the old stations and halts. Some had been turned into private residences, some coffee shops, and some simply decorated with flowers and lovingly tended by locals. The names of such stations are often fascinating. One that stood out on the Camel Trail was Grogley Halt. I just had to stop and get a selfie here!

After a while, we arrived at Wadebridge and cafes that were open! We got our bacon roll and Snoop was happy again.

Because of the issues yesterday with timings, I was cutting short my breaks to make sure I made good time, and I pushed on. The river and the paths were now much narrower, winding their way through scented pines and foxglove glades.

Just before Wenfordbridge, I met a local cyclist on his regular daily circuit.

'You going far with that load?'.

John O'Groats, but not today!'

He sidestepped my attempt at humour.

'Good luck with that, you'll need refuelling before you hit the moor. Stop at the Snail's Pace Café just up the hill and order the Ploughmans. It'll keep you going all afternoon' he said without taking a breath.

With that, he was off before I could say anything else.

'OK, thank you!' I shouted into the cloud of dust he'd created as he took off.

There were a couple of route options just along the path, and I assumed he must have known where I was going. My route took me directly to the Snail's Pace Café, which was a cabin at the end of the Camel Trail. They did food and hired out bikes. I sat outside and ordered a Ploughmans, as recommended, and a latte. Apart from the wasps who made a b-line for my pickle, it was very good!

It turned out to be a good refuelling decision considering that the flat terrain of the Camel trail had ended and I was heading uphill onto Bodmin Moor.

I was expecting an incline of impossible steepness from river level to moor level. The profile in Komoot went from flat for about twenty miles to a two-mile, orange-coloured incline at what seemed like forty-five degrees.

'You might need to get off and push Snoop…' He didn't look very pleased.

As it turned out the hill was steep, but not get-off-the-bike-and-push steep.

Bodmin Moor was an amazing place, rugged and exposed, with craggy outcrops, tors and narrow roads, A true wilderness. Some interesting names up here: Catshole, Butter's Tor, Hard Head, Rough Tor, and Brown Willy! Intriguing how place names come about, but not always easy to find out. I was so pleased the weather was so calm and pleasant, despite the persistent breeze from the east. It imagined it would be so different up here in bad weather.

A little further on and the cycle route zig zagged very oddly through an open airfield: RAF Davidstow. It was a little strange, the complete opposite of the moorland I had been cycling on with its winding roads. The roads here were completely straight and the landscape flat. I kept looking over my shoulder, half expecting an aircraft to appear on the horizon, or some military vehicle to speed past me.

It was last used as an airfield from late 1942 until 1945, and then became a motor racing circuit in the early 1950s. It was now populated by sheep and camper vans. It seemed that camper vans were starting to outnumber sheep in some areas.

I plodded on, uphill, downhill, uphill, downhill, uphill, downhill. I began to think 'Why am I doing this?'. This was more difficult than I had planned. I had been warned about the hills in Cornwall and Devon and heard about seasoned cyclists being reduced to tears and giving up in the first few days. I could now understand why. The weather for me was warm and dry, so I was fortunate. It's not easy to see this however when your legs don't want to keep going round & round and when your backside says, 'get me off this saddle!' Had it been wet and cold, I think I would have given up too.

The Sustrans book recommended diverting to Bude - 'A destination for bathers since the Victorian era' apparently, and it would have been lovely under any other circumstances, but I had to get off my saddle before my backside burst into flames.

Pushing on I passed through Bridgerule over the River Tamar and in doing so crossed from Cornwall into Devon.

I finally arrived at Goodworthy Campsite near Holsworthy at 5.30pm, surprised that I had made such good time. However I hadn't stopped much along the way, so the planned stops weren't working. If I had stopped for my full breaks, I would have arrived at least an hour later. However, I was finding that I perhaps didn't need as many stops, or at least stopping for as long wasn't needed. I would stop for photos, grab a snack from my bike bag, or stop for lunch as I did today at the Snail's Pace café, and stop for only 20 or 30 minutes. This was enough, and I was hoping that this might make up for my slower-than-planned pace.

This was a busy campsite with caravans, camper vans and tents. The owners were dealing with a few arrivals at once.

I was given a nice flat pitch not too far from the toilet block. £7 a night was a steal, but despite the low cost, it was clean & tidy. The sun was still shining, and the country air was fresh.

'Snoop, this is the life'. I took a deep breath, relieved that day three was complete.

Sue, one of the owners of the campsite, wandered over at about 6pm.

'We know that there are not many eating options around here for the likes of cyclists, and we're getting a Chinese take-away. Would you like anything?'

I was taken by surprise by her kind offer and probably should have accepted.

'That's really kind of you, but I have something to eat in the tent. Thank you so much, I appreciate you asking'.

I'm a bit of an idiot sometimes, my own worst enemy. I only had a tuna pot to eat. A Chicken Chow Mien would have gone down very nicely.

My default reaction to offers of help is often 'I can manage, thank you' or 'I've got this'. I think it comes from a combination of not being good at making quick decisions, plus a built-in independence. When I'm put in this position, I need time to process the question, so in this particular scenario, I couldn't really say 'I need to think about this, come back later'. She needed to know there and then, so I defaulted to the negative.

'Snoop I think it's your turn to make dinner tonight' He didn't bat an eyelid. Typical, I thought, don't know why I brought him along. So I had another tuna pot, whoopee!

Before the trip, I looked into eating and nutrition. Some blogs on the Internet told of cyclists who did LEJOG solely on cycling supplements and little else, so they weren't carrying the weight of food along the way. I thought in my infinite wisdom that 'I was going to eat better than that!' and figured I probably didn't need any special cycling nutrition supplements. Jelly Babies were recommended somewhere on the Internet as a good source of carbohydrates & protein to give a boost should I get a bit tired. I figured I could live on fish & chips, takeaways, and cooked breakfasts, supplemented by cold beans and tuna, cereal bars, and chocolate. Beans and tuna after all were high in protein too.... With the benefit of hindsight, I was way off the mark!

Eating on the go, in general, doesn't provide great nutrition. Fast food and takeaways are often full of fat, salt, and sugar. OK, high calories are probably good for cycling distances and to an extent are needed, but I was finding that my route didn't pass many places where I could buy takeaways anyway. I was hoping to pass chip shops regularly; fish is a great protein source, right? and the chips provided some good carbs, but I hadn't seen any chip shops at all so far.

My focus at this point however wasn't food, it was getting from A to B. My backside was not happy so I just kept peddling.

Despite the discomfort on the bike, I was starting to enjoy camping. Getting to camp each day was such a relief, and I was getting into a routine.

With the tent out of the rucksack, it took me less than 10 minutes to put it up. The routine then was chuck all the bags in the tent, unroll the sleeping mat and blow it up, unroll the sleeping bag, blow up my inflatable pillow, and head for a wash or shower.

Although sometimes I didn't wash or shower, it depended on how clean the facilities looked. I was also aware that England was more of a Covid hotspot than Scotland at this time, so I was very careful when using shared facilities. I'm not sure what I would have done if I'd caught Covid. How can you self-isolate on a campsite for the recommended 10 days? So washing wasn't a big priority if the site was busy, or if it didn't appear clean.

In the tent, I had a place for everything, which helped in the middle of the night when fumbling in the dark for stuff.

This was a busy site, probably due to the low-cost pitches, so I didn't use the facilities, although they appeared to be very clean. I lay in the tent, not quite as exhausted as yesterday but tired, nonetheless.

'Snoop, who's idea was this?' I questioned. Yesterday was a shock to the system, and I wasn't sure I was going the be able to keep this up for 20 days.

I had always enjoyed cycling, but this was on a different level, and in this moment, I wasn't really enjoying it. I lay in the tent and reminisced about the times I did enjoy cycling.

I had bikes as a kid and into my teens when my pride and joy was a bright blue Raleigh Chopper, the coolest bike of the 1970s, with high handlebars, a motorbike-style gear lever and an elongated saddle. But in reality, it was a seriously flawed bike and very uncomfortable on anything but a short ride. Certainly not a serious bike for a long journey.

In my early twenties, living on the west coast of Scotland at Wemyss Bay, I bought a Raleigh Elite, a pretty normal run-around with flat bars. I was never into, what we called at the time, racing bikes with drop bars. They're now simply called road bikes. I wasn't a serious cyclist by any means and didn't participate in any kind of cycling club or group. This was mainly due to working in catering and only having a Thursday off work. No weekend cycle tours with a cycling club for me. So my choice of bike was a more practical decision and not influenced by others. As a result, my cycles were mostly solo efforts.

Perhaps the most memorable excursion from this time was a 36-mile circular cycle around the north of the Isle of Arran with my younger sister, who I called Bean. She called me Jean. (I can't remember why). The Isle of Arran, off the west coast of Scotland, accessed by a one-hour ferry trip, was often called Scotland in miniature due to the low-lying South Island and the Highland-like north. The island had a road all the way around, plus a road across the middle that climbed to 750 feet at its highest point. We cycled north from the ferry, completing an anti-clockwise circuit of the island's north, returning over the String, as the middle road was called.

I remember us hurtling down the hill from the road's summit to sea level at Brodick to catch the ferry. Bean was going far too fast, and as I tried to keep up with her, my bike juddered and shook so much that it was all I could do to keep it on the road.

'Slow down Bean!'.

I shouted as loud as I could, but my voice was lost in the wind rush and she just seemed to go faster. Young and carefree, we didn't even own cycle helmets. Fortunately, we lived to tell the tale, and get the boat back to the mainland!

By my mid-twenties, life's responsibilities took over with marriage, children, and work. More leisurely activities got pushed to one side. I only renewed my love of cycling, after a lot of life's water had gone under the bridge, at the age of forty-eight.

Happy memories as I drifted off to sleep.

Miles of Memories

Day four - The Only Way is Up

I woke up to a heavy dew again. The outer tent and the bike were dripping wet, but the sky was clear and the sun was about to peek over the horizon, hopefully, another glorious day was in store. I had just about run out of food but had a big tin of baked beans and pork sausages, so this was breakfast, cold straight from the tin, as usual, just the way I liked them!

I was thinking about the planning I had done based on the Sustrans book and was beginning to have doubts.

As mentioned previously; to create a cycling plan I carefully mapped the route from the book into Komoot initially in sixty-mile sections. Komoot was good in that it gave you a breakdown of the route you had mapped based on your fitness level and the terrain you were covering. Once you had plotted the route, it gave you the projected time to complete each section, distance, average speed, uphill and downhill, rise and fall, plus the elevation profile and a breakdown of the way types and surfaces you would be cycling on.

Over a period of months, I tweaked the route to match where I would camp and settled on what I thought would be a good daily balance depending on the terrain. I also factored in two nights in Penzance and two nights in Thurso, giving me more time to linger at the start and end of the journey. This also meant I could travel light on the day to Land's End and the day to John O'Groats. I had done as much as I could without being out there at ground level and seeing what I would be cycling on. I knew there were going to be some unknowns and I just had to accept that.

Well, I was now finding the unknowns. But the trouble was rerouting at this stage at best wasn't going to help much, and at worst could see me ending up on very busy roads.

I packed up and headed off from the Goodworthy campsite setting Komoot to navigate to my next destination.

The route today would see me heading east initially, then north and east to Bideford and Barnstaple, before swinging north again to Loxhore and my next campsite, before the big climb up Exmoor.

Komoot was still guiding me, and the app itself was pretty good as a satnav, however, it had a few drawbacks in practical use through the phone app. I thought it would be a good idea to run Komoot on a separate phone from the phone I would use for taking photos and making calls. This allowed me to fix my 'satnav phone' to the handlebars where it could remain undisturbed. This part worked great.

To maximise the phone's battery power, the screen could be set to come on only when a turn was necessary. This didn't work so well, either some turns were missed as the screen didn't always come on, or it came on at the very last second. Either way, it meant a few wrong turns. This wasn't too bad in the countryside where the route choices were either obvious or few, but in towns and cities it slowed me right down, and I took quite a few wrong turns.

To counter this I would hit the power button to turn the screen on just before a possible route change, plus I turned on voice navigation. Even so, Kamoot's ability to identify turns was a bit hit-and-miss, so I had to be vigilant rather than relying totally on the app.

All this added up to slower progress and this was the main reason that my planned routes were taking longer than expected. On my training days at home, I knew the routes in my local area and I could zip along quite happily without being held back. In planning, I didn't factor in unfamiliar roads and paths!

And so was the case as I left Goodworthy campsite. I took a wrong turn and strayed quite a way off the route before I realised it. I finally ended up back on my route in the town of Holsworthy, after a very roundabout way, where I stopped at a BP garage for some food supplies.

'Got a bike load there, you 'ave. Where you off to?'

Here we go again. A guy dressed in black emerged from the garage shop and was looking over my bike. I gave him the John O'Groats story.

'Had a friend who tried that. Didn't make it, he didn't'

'Oh, what happened' I enquired.

'Got knocked off his bike, he did. Ended up in hospital poor chap'

'Oh dear, hope he was ok?' By the grave tones of his voice, I was expecting him to say he was still in a coma or something.

'Pulled through fine, he did, but vowed to never do it again.'

I set off again a little more depressed than I was when I stopped.

I was now in Devon; the Cornwall box was well and truly ticked, and it dawned on me that I had completely failed in my quest to have a Cornish Pasty in Cornwall.

The good news was that today was a little shorter and the elevations were not quite as high, so I tried to look on the bright side. I was still cycling into a light breeze, but the sun was out and it was warm but not too warm. Pretty ideal for cycling.

As I cycled along the remote country roads, many places along the way had little stalls outside with local produce and honesty boxes to drop your cash into. The usual items were eggs, but I saw stalls with seasonal vegetables and even jars of pickles and jam and home baking.

I passed through Bradford. No not Bradford, Yorkshire, but Bradford, Devon, and a field of very orange cows. I was now cycling parallel to the River Torridge and in a dip in the road, floodplain markers indicated how deep the water might get. I was so glad that my route through here wasn't on a rainy day.

I reached Sheepwash. This sounded like a good place to stop if you had a sheep and it needed a wash. I didn't have a sheep, but Snoop did look a bit sheepish (in more ways than one). He wasn't up for it though. He threw me a look that said, 'Don't be stupid Alan'

It turned out that the name Sheepwash was first documented in 1166 and unsurprisingly was a place where sheep were washed before shearing. No beating about the bush here!

Great name for a village though. They obviously called a spade a spade around here. It made me smile imagining living here and someone asking, 'Oh I live in Sheepwash!'. Love it!

The valleys and hills rolled by stunning countryside.

'Look Snoop' I motioned to a field with pretty yellow flowers 'There's a field of Devon Custard'. I deserved the silent treatment for that one.

Shortly I reached a gate and stile onto a gravel path, which headed off in a straight line into the distance. An info board said 'The Tarka Trail'. This was another disused railway, a 180-mile-long circular cycleway through the north Devonshire countryside. I wouldn't be doing the full circuit, my route took me on the trail for 30 miles, most of which was downhill.

Along the trail were mosaic statues; giant statues covered in tiny tiles. One looked like it must be Tarka the Otter himself, but at an oversized 12-foot high and quite overbearing, he was intimidatingly scary.

Being a Sunday, everyone and their granny were out on the trail, so progress was a little slow, but the downhill was great, and I managed, in passing, to get a latte in a cycle café – a disused station house.

The rail bridges over the River Torridge provided spectacular views down the valley with people enjoying boating and canoeing.

On one of the bridges, some cyclists had stopped and were pointing downstream. As you do when people are pointing at something, you feel compelled to stop and have a look too. A girl kneeling on a paddleboard was making her way down the river and at first glance she looked completely naked, but on second glance, she had a near-body-colour swimsuit on. The second glance: I'm sure someone said to me 'The second glance is the killer, don't do it'. So I'd failed today, but at least this particular second glance didn't lead me astray.

The Landcross tunnel appeared, the railway track finding its way through a ridge between the Rivers Yeo and Torridge, and I went from bright sunlight to what seemed like near darkness. Fortunately, there were occasional lights on the tunnel roof throwing pools of illumination onto where the train track would have run. I found myself making steam train noises as I chugged through.

'Woo woooo' I shouted as I emerged from the darkness. Snoop was looking the other way in embarrassment.

Bideford appeared at the bottom of the hill with its salt marshes and the smell of the sea. The long winding cycle path tracked the wide River Torridge estuary continuing past more sections of preserved railway and the Bideford Railway Heritage Centre. Now I'm not a rail enthusiast, but it would have been nice to stop and explore, but I had to push on.

After Bideford and the river outlet to the Atlantic, the cycleway tracked the River Taw inland and eastwards towards Barnstaple. I approached a busy café at Fremington Quay overlooking the river, another disused stationhouse and railway platform by the look of it. People were sauntering along with ice cream cones and the smell of bacon wafted down the cycle path. My stomach started to rumble, but the queue was out of the café and down the side of the building. If only it wasn't Sunday, it might not have been so busy. I pushed on to Barnstaple in the hope of finding somewhere to eat.

Barnstaple on a Sunday after 4pm. The cafes had closed, and the takeaways hadn't opened, so I ended up at a Brewers Fayre type place just beyond the main town in Newport. On the door, it said 'Bookings Only', but people were sitting outside with drinks, and I hoped they might take pity on this bedraggled lone cyclist. I went inside to find out. The place wasn't busy, was this a promising sign?

A waitress appeared, 'Hello, I'm looking for something to eat. I'm by myself' I announced.

'Have you booked?'

'No'

'Sorry we're only doing bookings'

'Can I book just now then'

'When for?'

'Erm, well for just now, or as soon as possible….'

'Sorry we're fully booked today – short staffed I'm afraid'

I left the half-empty restaurant. I guess Covid was taking its toll. I was running out of options, and I knew that this was the final stop for getting anything to eat as I was heading out of the built-up areas.

I ended up at Whiddon Valley Stores a short distance away, a corner shop, where I purchased more baked beans, a couple of sandwiches, and more Jelly Babies. Opposite the shop was the Whiddon Valley Frier. A chip shop! – it was closed on a Sunday – of course.

The remaining part of the journey was on country roads and through villages heading uphill towards Exmoor.

Finding a place to stay around here was one of the bigger issues I had when planning the trip. Sixty miles landed me right in the middle of Exmoor, and I considered wild camping when I got there, but thought better of it due to it being illegal in England. Although I wouldn't have left any trace, I just knew that I wouldn't have been at ease that night and would have been alert to every noise outside the tent.

'Is that the farmer coming to chuck me off his field?'.

So I eventually found a campsite two miles off my route just short of Exmoor.

The route to the campsite from Barnstaple seemed a bit steep when viewing the profile in Komoot, so I decided to take a more round-about route. The logic was that although it was longer, it would be a gentler incline.

As it turned out it *was* a gentler incline until I had to divert off my route at Bratton Fleming. Komoot directed me to Mill Lane, the road to Loxhore where the campsite was.

I was heading downhill again and had a bad feeling about this. The road narrowed to a single track with grass down the middle, and it wound down the hill at an ever-increasing gradient for a mile. I had to cycle back up this hill tomorrow!

'Noooooo…. You stupid idiot!' I shouted at myself as I careered down the steep hill which seemed never-ending. Snoop was covering his eyes at the speed and rate of the descent.

At the bottom, I had lost 500ft and was horrified that all my uphill effort was wasted, but this wasn't the end, I was at the bottom of a valley and still had a mile to go to get to the campsite which was inevitably uphill from here. I pushed my bike up the final mile. This hill seemed even steeper than the downhill, but I was too out of breath to complain, instead, I muttered under my breath,

'Snoop there is no way we are cycling back down here tomorrow!'

This was probably the steepest hill that I experienced on the whole trip.

Two miles to completely undo my gentle incline plan! I obviously hadn't looked closely enough at the elevation in Komoot. Worse still, I knew that tomorrow I had to go back the same two miles along the same road and tackle the other side of the hill, before even getting back to my route start point in Bratton Fleming and continuing uphill onto Exmoor. I felt so stupid that I hadn't spotted this.

The direct cycle from Barnstaple would have been half the elevation, and six miles shorter. I didn't know how, but I had to get back to Bratton Fleming avoiding the plunge down this valley. In a big taxi? or on a tractor? Was there a different route?

I recounted my sorry tale to Julie, the site owner at the North town Farm campsite and she confirmed that I had taken an awfully long way around. I asked her if there was anyone who could run me with the bike back to my route the next morning. I was willing to pay for a suitably sized taxi or something, rather than tackle that hill. In the back of my mind was the fact that the next day was already one of the longer cycles of the whole trip, and to add on this extra mileage and elevation just to get back to the start of my route might just tip me over the edge. Thankfully, she said she should be able to arrange for some help.

North town Farm was lovely and very peaceful with pitches well spread around the edge of a large clean grassy field. The grass had mostly been allowed to grow tall, and furrows were mown into the field providing paths to the pitching locations. Beautifully basic as they describe themselves on their website.

They were big on recycling and eco-friendly, with separate bins for everything, and the quirky toilets in particular were very off-grid. These seemed to be hand-built from wood, with a toilet seat over a hole in the floor. Gents were asked to sit for even a number one, as pee and poo were captured in separate receptacles, and organically disposed of.

'How about that for a job Snoop?' He turned away in disgust at the thought of it. It didn't bear thinking about, but I guess life on a farm was probably full of similarly unpleasant jobs.

Later I heard a voice from outside the tent:

'Hi, there'. I popped my head out of the tent. Julie's husband stood outside. I guess knocking on a tent door doesn't work.

'Oh hello, you must be Paul'.

I was just back from having a shower and still dripping wet.

'Julie can run you back to Bratton Fleming in the morning in our pickup'

'That's amazing. You're a lifesaver! Thank you', I was so relieved.

He asked me about my cycle, and I gave him the usual well-rehearsed spiel. He wished me luck.

I didn't ask, but guessed, that as they were quite far north in Devon, they didn't get many LEJOGers staying with them. Later after returning home and reviewing the route, I imagine more sensible LEJOGers would choose to skirt south of the heights of Exmoor instead of going over the top of it as I intended to.

The evening sun was setting on the farm and the last rays caught the tops of the long grass as it swayed in the breeze. It was very peaceful and I could have stayed here several nights.

Mrs B heard all about my exploits today and made all the right noises to comfort me. This was turning into a challenge and a half. All the planning in the world couldn't have helped me to cope with this, and tomorrow was looking like another tough day.

'Snoop, get a good night's sleep tonight – we have a marathon cycle tomorrow and I'll need your help'.

Typically, he didn't respond. He was in a world of his own transfixed by the movement of the tall grass.

Exhaustion set in, and I was soon asleep.

Day five - A Place to Hideaway

Another early rise - my departures were getting earlier and earlier! I had agreed to meet up with Julie in their farmyard at 7am for the lift back to my route. On the way, I spotted the farm's glorious cattle herd, a group of Devon Ruby Reds, with coats of dark red-brown. They watched me as I passed the gate to their field.

Julie was waiting for me when I arrived in the farmyard, and we got my bike into the back of her pickup. It took no time at all to drive down the hill and back up the other side. If I had tackled this on the bike it would have taken a lot longer pushing the bike up that steep hill.

On the journey, she recounted the story of a family on bikes who found themselves in a similar predicament as me and were stranded on the wrong side of the valley. I felt a little better that I wasn't the only one who had been caught out.

Julie wouldn't take any money for the lift, so I thanked her, psyched myself up for the challenging day ahead, and continued uphill towards Exmoor.

Today was looking like a long haul at a planned 75 miles. However, once over Exmoor the second half of the journey appeared to be quite flat. I was pretty much heading east all day, through Dulverton, Bampton, Taunton and Bridgwater to my campsite near Stawell.

I was meeting a good friend Alireza in Taunton, who moved to the nearby village of Chard for employment, so I had to make sure I was on time for this.

Exmoor rose before me at 7.15am, and a coffee would have been good for a caffeine boost as I approached the hills. I had eaten yet another tin of beans for breakfast, so I guess jet propulsion might have been on the cards, but failing this I just got my head down and kept pedalling.

That irritating east wind picked up again as I cycled towards the plateau of the moor. Approaching the top, I looked back over Devon and wondered if I was able to see as far back as Cornwall. Probably not, but I could see a long way. The rolling hills and valleys fell before me and I stared transfixed by the beauty and peace of the landscape, Chef Snoopy was equally transfixed as he stared ahead in silence. The sheep in a nearby field were looking at us suspiciously. I knew what they were thinking.

'There's another one of those idiot humans on a two-wheeled contraption. He should have stuck to four wheels'.

I had questions for them. 'What's this wind about? Isn't the prevailing wind supposed to be from the west?'.

They looked up and gave me a blank stare. I don't think they cared. They thought I was mad - I thought I was mad! Why am I doing this? I'd given myself an almost impossible deadline today.

The highest point on the road over Exmoor was 1750 ft. This was at the top of the initial incline, and once here, the landscape took a downward trajectory as I exited Devon and entered Somerset. Two counties now under my belt, it was a good feeling.

It was exposed and windy, a little chilly, but at least it wasn't raining, and there was beauty in the moorland wildness. The panoramic views were spectacular as the broken clouds skimmed the moor, and rolled over the landscape, the light constantly changing minute by minute as the pockets of sun and shadow shifted. The inclines over the plateau were gentle rather than steep, making cycling very pleasurable, and as there was only really one road to follow, I could zip along making what I thought was a good time. Later I would realise I wasn't making a good time at all.

On the far side of the moor, I saw groups of horses trotting along and grazing. It was nice to see the animals in a wild habitat with plenty of space to roam. It crossed my mind that they might be Exmoor Ponies, but I doubted myself as I wasn't sure there was such a thing. I'd heard of Dartmoor Ponies... I later found out that they were indeed Exmoor ponies, and that records of ponies on Exmoor go back to 1086.

'Snoop, what's the difference between a pony and a horse?'

Like he would know, but I asked anyway. He thought about it for a long, long time but eventually came up with nothing. Looking it up later, Mr Google said that it's the size that decides. Below a certain number of hands, it's a pony, otherwise, it's a horse.

'Just the right size for you Snoop' I could see him galloping along holding on to the reins. Not sure he agreed, but I didn't expect him to.

Leaving the moor behind was with mixed emotions. It had a wild untouched beauty and the slightly chillier air was fresh, but I was looking forward to getting something to eat in a café somewhere. It was four hours into the day and I'd cycled this on a single tin of beans. I was thinking an all-day breakfast and a latte would go down a treat.

The road headed predominantly downhill to Dulverton, and as I rolled into the village it instantly captured me by its charm. A popular tourist destination, it had history by the bucketload. However, after hours in the saddle, I was determined to hunt down my breakfast and latte, which I found at the Copper Kettle Café.

At the café, there was nowhere to lock up my bike outside, but I spotted that the café had a garden with seating at the back. However, the shops were terraced and I couldn't see a way around them. I popped my head in the door.

'Excuse me, can I get around the back with my bike?'

'Hello lovely, no way around, just bring it through'

So I picked up my bike and carried it through the closely packed café tables.

'Erm excuse me please' I needed someone to pull their chair in to let me past. 'Thank you!'

'Oops sorry' I think I startled an elderly lady as she turned around, nearly choking on her scone. Snoop thought it was hilarious, so I clipped him around the ear.

I made it to the garden and waited for my brunch. Real food. It was delicious! I was beginning to realise that I hadn't planned my cycling nutrition very well at all.

I was now raring to go but had to negotiate my way back through the café, which was now even busier. I felt like shouting 'Man & bike coming through!' but I was a little more polite than this.

I was aware that I was meeting Alireza in Taunton, and I calculated my ETA and messaged him:

'Should we aim for 3pm at Costa?' We agreed on the time and place and I set off again.

I pushed on now, knowing I had to be at a certain place at a certain time, cycling along mostly country lanes towards Taunton. A few more typically English villages flashed past with narrow streets and chocolate box houses, and although the terrain started quite flat, the occasional hill took me by surprise.

On reflection, looking at the route profile in Komoot later in the day, the height of Exmoor had minimised the scale of the second part of the journey, making the hills look smaller than they actually were.

Passing through Bampton, NCN3 took a big diversion south to Tiverton, and then back north again, but my route continued east on NCN344 for 10 miles before rejoining NCN3.

'Nice shortcut Snoop!'. He agreed for once and we pushed on as fast as we could to meet our deadline.

Two hours into my Taunton trek I realised I wasn't making as good time as I thought I would, and I recalculated to arrive at about 4pm.

I messaged Alireza.

'Alireza! I just recalculated and it will be closer to 4pm. Really sorry. Is this OK?'

It was 1pm and I felt bad about pushing the time back. It was OK, of course, it had to be OK as I couldn't get there any sooner.

Iranian-born Alireza was a good guy, very patient and calm, a true gentleman. We previously worked together and he was one of the most reliable and honest people I had met, it would be an honour just to meet up with him again.

As I neared Taunton, I cycled through a feature in the landscape called Nynehead Hollow. This was a deep sandstone gorge with rock faces on either side which looked totally natural. However, I believe it was dug out by a local landowner in the nineteenth century to improve local access. Impressive, nonetheless.

I was pedalling even more furiously now and on arriving in Taunton switched to Google Maps to get me from my planned route to the Costa, which was in a retail park a couple of miles off-route. After getting around some unexpected roadworks I finally arrived at 4.15pm. Alireza was in good form and we chatted and caught up for about 45 minutes. Unfortunately, I still had two more hours of cycling, so I had to be off again to make it before it got dark.

My cycle legs and backside were certainly being tested again today and I set off pedalling like crazy along the canal between Taunton and Bridgwater. Thankfully, the hills were behind me now; these last few miles were very flat.

At Bridgwater, I passed over the canal and onto country roads towards my stop for the night. The light was fading as I arrived at The Hideaway campsite just after 7pm, twelve hours after setting off in the morning.

The place had a few camper vans, caravans, and a couple of tents, but nobody was to be seen, no reception area, and no indication of where to go. Do I just go in and camp? Then I noticed the coded locks on the toilet block. I needed to find someone.

'What now Snoop?'. I looked over at him for an answer, but he didn't know either.

There were two houses on-site, fenced off and out-of-bounds to campers. I figured the owners must live here, so I trespassed into the garden of the first house and knocked on the door. A little old lady in her dressing gown (or house coat as Mrs B would call it) opened the door a small crack.

'Sorry to disturb you, but I'm booked into the campsite and no one is around'.

She didn't look very sure of me, and I wondered if she might slam the door shut, leaving me standing.

'My daughter runs the site; does she know you're coming?' she said.

I'd booked this site online, and Jill the owner insisted on me paying the fees upfront by bank transfer. After paying online, she emailed me as if I hadn't paid, saying I needed to pay if they were to reserve the pitch. After a couple of emails back and forth, she found my payment.

I had visions of being turned away and trying to find somewhere else. Maybe my booking had been lost again?

'She does know I'm coming; I have an email from her', I pulled out my mobile to show her the email….

'I'll call her' she announced and closed the door

'I'll just wait out at the entrance to the site then?' I said to the closed door. I thought this might be a good idea, so I retreated to the campsite entrance. I guessed that either someone would come out, or a police car would turn up with sirens blaring.

'We might have to just camp Snoop, even if we can't access the toilets….' I looked around for a suitable clump of trees or bushes that might provide cover should I have to resort to nature.

At that moment, a friendly man appeared and came over to greet me.

'Sorry for your wait, I'm Glen, let me get you sorted out'.

He was most helpful. I asked him about recharging my mobile phones or the possibility of paying a bit extra for an electric hook-up, but he hooked me up without charging any extra.

In preparation for the trip, I wired up a short extension cable with a standard 3-pin trailing socket on one end and an outdoor-type plug on the other which would connect to the standard outdoor socket used on campsites. This connected nicely with the outdoor socket on-site.

The site had a drying room and a microwave oven in one of the huts, which was great as I was having problems getting my towel dry, so the drying room was perfect.

'Do you like porridge?' Glen asked. 'I'll leave you some oats in a bowl by the microwave for breakfast'.

Honestly, he couldn't do enough to help me, and this turned out to be the best campsite of the whole trip.

My plans for keeping my phones topped up with charge were to take two rechargeable power packs with me. These devices, as stated in their advertising, would recharge a phone fully six times. In reality, they would recharge a partially charged phone about 4 or 5 times to 100%. One of them had a solar panel on top to assist with the recharge of the pack. I had visions of strapping it to the top of my rucksack and it could charge up as I cycled. However, the charging ability of the solar panel was barely faster than a speeding snail, so hardly worth it.

I left home with them fully charged (from the mains), and topped them up in Penzance, so I'd been charging my phones from these power packs for four days and both were running close to empty. Therefore, the electric hook-up at this site was very welcome, and I recharged both power packs and phones overnight. This turned out to be timely as I wouldn't be able to recharge any devices for another four days after this.

After today's marathon cycle or triple marathon, if a marathon is 26 miles, I was whacked. I called Mrs B for my usual check-in and probably didn't make much sense as I was so tired, and then I was out like a light.

Miles of Memories

Day six - New Age : New Roads

With a sigh of relief, I woke knowing that today's route was shorter and at a lower elevation, but I was a little sore and drained from the 75 miles yesterday. Today would be a contrast, I had a few 'famous' places to pass through: Glastonbury, Wells, the Mendips, and Bristol, all on a north-east trajectory. But first breakfast.

Glen was true to his word and I found a bowl of porridge oats by the microwave. It was amazing to have a warm breakfast – porridge & banana! Yum!!. I had porridge every morning at home with banana, blueberries, walnuts, and soya milk, and I was missing this as a start to the day.

I packed everything up and was soon ready to head off, but I couldn't find my specs anywhere. I searched everywhere I'd been since the previous evening, but they were nowhere to be found.

'Snoop, have you seen them? Or have you *hidden* them?' I said accusingly. He's a little rascal sometimes. He gave me that wide-eyed look which said, 'Who me?'

I had my prescription sunglasses, so these would have to do until I could unpack all my bags and check again. As usual, nobody else was up and about as I left. It would have been nice to say a proper thank you to Glen & Jill but it wasn't meant to be. I needed to leave a review on their website.

The sky was overcast today, and the persistent east wind was a little stronger than on previous days. I was cycling right into it which slowed me down a little, but there's always a positive. An east wind is often a dry wind. And so far it hadn't rained on me at all!

Glastonbury wasn't far away and after about an hour I rolled into the main street. The cafés were just opening and people were sitting outside with breakfasts and coffees. I got a takeaway latte. Had it been lunchtime I would have stopped for an all-day breakfast, but I was still full after the porridge. A market was on in one of the car parks selling crafts and foods, the usual market fayre.

Glastonbury was known as a 'spiritual' centre, shops named, 'Man, Myth and Magik' and 'Cat & Cauldron' kind of summed up the New Age atmosphere found here. Even the town's website, Glastonbury Online, summed up that this place was not your run-of-the-mill town:

'Welcome to Glastonbury, possibly the quirkiest town in England. Steeped in history, myth, and the smell of incense'.

Glastonbury Tor loomed over the town. Now in the care of the National Trust, apparently it was the home of Gwyn ap Nudd, the Lord of the Underworld, and a place where the fairy folk lived. Enough said!

'Snoop, I think we need to get out of here', I said. I'm sure I saw him nodding but it was possibly a trick on the light.

The atmosphere in the place freaked us both out a bit. Even Komoot was confused and refused to direct me through the town. Later on, when reviewing the route that Komoot had plotted, it had lost its GPS in the town. There was definitely something a little strange with this place: disruption of the magnetic fields or lay lines? I didn't hang around to find out and was quickly on my way towards Wells and the Mendips.

Wells, its population of about 12,000, was a short distance away, the smallest city in England (St David's in Wales holds the title of the smallest city in the UK). It oozed old English charm and had some very impressive architecture, including the famous thirteenth-century Gothic Cathedral, the moated Medieval Bishop's Palace, Vicars' Close, St Cuthbert's Church and a good local museum. The whole city covered just two square miles. I didn't stay long, as usual, I had to press on – I had seen where I was going next – a big hill!

Just before the climb up into the Mendips I came across Wookey Hole and thought I had cycled into the entrance to Disneyland. An ice cream parlour, café and shops were backed by a fairytale-style hotel complete with a turret, and there were lots of kids! It was quite unexpected. The signs said Wookey Hole Resort.

The main attraction was the Wookey Hole Caves, a series of limestone caverns around which other tourist attractions had been built. I didn't linger – too many screaming kids – it was after all the school summer holidays.

Snoop wanted to stay and explore, but I told him no. He's a big kid at heart.

The Mendips rose above me, a chunk of hills in the middle of my otherwise flat route, a 1000ft plateau, 10 miles across, and I knew there was a steep climb coming. I wasn't wrong, and it was another episode of get-off-the-bike-and-push. The good thing about the Mendips was that it was steep up, a flat(ish) top, and steep down. So after the climb up, it was plain sailing for a good stretch.

I had been mostly on NCN3 since Land's End and heading north-east. However, at Chew Stoke, I left NCN3 behind and joined NCN334, and then NCN33 into Bristol crossing my third county boundary.

As I headed for Bristol the terrain got flatter. The city, with its prosperous maritime history, straddled the River Avon.

The route took me directly to the docks where huge cranes lined the harbour and nineteenth-century warehouses contained modern restaurants and shops; a glimpse of the industrial past where now much restoration and re-appropriation of buildings had taken place.

It was quite busy at the docks and I didn't want to hang about. Although I planned to stop and get something to eat somewhere, the opportunity didn't appear.

In a city or big town, my security radar kicked in and I was much more reluctant to just park up the bike and go into a shop or café, even though I had a good strong lock.

The harbour was filled with trendy bars and shops, but a burger van or some other kind of street food would have been ideal. I could have stood with the bike waiting: bacon, eggs, sausage on a nice crispy roll. My mouth was watering just thinking about it. No sauce thanks. Eggs and tomato sauce are a no-no for me! There was no such thing, nowhere where I could just order something from the street. So, I moved through swiftly.

The Sustrans route in the book took the cyclist on a north-west route out of Bristol, heading towards, then running parallel to, the River Severn, the longest river in the UK. However I needed to find a campsite just beyond the city, and they appeared to be few and far between. The best I could do was a campsite inland, ten miles north-east near Chipping Sodbury. Cycle routes were available both ways, so I diverted my route along the old Bristol & Bath Railway Path, designated as NCN4, which was flat and straight and quite busy with cyclists. It was late afternoon and I guess the start of the rush hour.

This was an ideal path for a commute into and back out of the city. Like many railways in cities, the route was set lower than the surrounding landscape, the city roads crisscrossing the railway path on bridges overhead. The disadvantage was that I didn't see anything more of Bristol itself; the path stretched to the edge of the city.

NCN4 eventually led onto the Bristol & Gloucester Railway path and I was back into the countryside picking my way through to Chipping Sodbury, and my next campsite.

Just how I got this far in my journey on the meagre rations I'd been living on was surprising. I seemed to have become blinkered to stopping and eating, and a grim determination had come over me to push on to get to my next destination no matter what.

And so it was through Chipping Sodbury. I must have passed several pubs, restaurants, and take-away places, but I didn't stop, despite being desperately hungry. My mind was set on getting to camp.

'Get to the campsite, then think about food'. I guess my humble logic was saying that once I'd got to the site it was one less unknown to think about.

I was now in Gloucestershire. Wold Camping was along a gated private-looking lane on the common beyond Chipping Sodbury. It turned out to be a field with a toilet block and a large wooden building which was called the 'Gathering Barn'. This was open on one side with tables, chairs, a small kitchen area and several shelves with books and board games.

A sign gave the owner's number with instructions to call on arrival. I called but got no answer, so left a message.

Several camper vans were parked up, and a few static tents lined part of the field. Each had a fire pit and some people had lit fires; smoke billowed over the site. There was plenty of room in the field and no marked plots, so I just picked a spot by a fence, upwind from the smoke trails, where I could lock up the bike. I pitched my tent and unpacked my bags.

It had been a dull day today, the skies overcast, the places I'd been through seemed a bit dark and foreboding, and then I realised I still had my prescription sunglasses on. Ah, that'll be why!

Climbing into the tent I found my regular specs in one of the inside pockets of the tent. One of the arms bent to an odd angle; it had been squashed as I rolled up in the tent in the morning. Chef Snoopy rolled his eyes but I tried to ignore him. I bent the glasses back into shape and was relieved that tomorrow would be a brighter day.

I hadn't had much to eat and was very hungry. I figured I might need to go back to Chipping Sodbury and find a fish & chip shop or get a food delivery if anyone came out this far. It was only two miles. In the Gathering Barn was a list of local eateries, so I phoned a chip shop and a Chinese restaurant.

'Do you deliver?'

'Sorry we don't'

The campsite owner, Babs, called back to say she was coming to the site. When she arrived, she briefed me on what I'd found out myself anyway, but I sought her advice on food.

'Could you recommend somewhere to eat around here – not too far away?

'Dominos deliver…. ' she said, and my face must have lit up. I was having visions of an enormous pizza with toppings galore. Chef Snoopy was ecstatic too and danced around the camp field in his own motionless way. This had to be seen to be believed.

A rather tasty pizza arrived half an hour later with an undisclosed number of toppings, garlic & herb dip and a bottle of Pepsi Max. Snoop and I sat in the Gathering Barn and demolished it, it was amazingly delicious and seemed like the best pizza we had ever tasted. On reflection, I guess having cycled myself close to starvation may have made it taste a little better.

It was probably today when I realised that this was not a sightseeing trip. In planning, I had envisioned all that I would see along the way, the amazing British countryside, the seascapes, the big cities, the history, and quaint villages. Although I had experienced some of this, the city and town routes, such as through Glastonbury and Bristol were a little disappointing. In reality, my main focus was getting to my planned destination for that day, and in doing that, I needed to keep moving and had very little time to stop and sightsee. It was pretty obvious in hindsight, although the sightseeing part was meant to be shoehorned into my 15-minute hourly breaks and the one-hour lunch break. As explained, these breaks weren't working out at all. In addition, although the Sustrans routes passed through several stunning locations, the routes through towns and cities didn't pass by the main city sights, so many famous locations that you might see on holiday in those areas were bypassed, unseen. Perhaps in planning, I should have identified more of the things I wanted to see and planned my route to pass them instead of sticking to the Sustrans route. – next time maybe, should there be a next time!

After checking in with Mrs B, I slept well with a full stomach that night and probably a huge grin on my face.

Day seven - Follow the Severn

I was getting used to this camping thing, so after a peaceful night and a good night's sleep, I was raring to go. 67 miles today, but one of the flattest routes of the whole trip.

My bike was performing well. I had purchased it only a few months previously with LEJOG in mind. It was a Genesis Tour de Fer, bought through the Cycle to Work Scheme. This was the most expensive bike I'd ever purchased, and I was hoping at the time that it was worth it.

Certainly, Genesis Bikes had a good reputation and the guy in the bike shop commented it was an 'awesome piece of kit'. But then he *was* trying to sell it to me. However, I had done my research before even approaching the shop, so I already knew it was awesome. Put it this way, it was the most I'd ever spent on a bike, so it had better be awesome! It was a purpose-built touring bike with disc brakes, a rack, mudguards, three bottle holders and puncture-protected tyres. This would be my first bike with disc brakes, which was exciting for me, but likely boring for everyone else. I bought spare brake pads just in case I wore them out with the mileage I was going to cover. I already had a Topeak rack bag with fold-out panniers and a small Topeak handlebar bag for valuables, which easily unclipped if I needed to take it into a shop or wherever.

A phone pouch with a see-through cover sat on the top bar to hold my sat-nav phone. I used an old phone specifically for this purpose. On my back was a medium-large 40ltr rucksack to hold my tent, sleeping bag, pillow and sleeping mat. Lastly were bottles in the bottle cages, two water bottles, and one bottle-shaped toolkit holder. The toolkit contained spare inner tubes, a pump, a chain tool, a multitool, tie wraps, spare bolts, spray lube, tyre levers and a puncture repair kit. Most of which I'd gathered from the experience of previous cycling commutes and expeditions.

My morning routine included a check over the bike and a spray of oil to keep the chain running smoothly.

The only problem I'd had with the bike so far was with the kickstand.

When purchasing the bike, the shop recommended a heavy-duty kickstand for touring. And indeed it was proving its worth. On previous bikes, when stopping, you would need to find something convenient to lean the bike against or lay it on the ground. Although maybe not very cool for some people, having a kickstand, allowed you to stop anywhere, flip the stand down, and prop the bike up to stand on its own. This was especially useful considering the weight of the bike with all the attached luggage.

The problem with the kickstand was that the retaining bolt had come loose a couple of times, and it had started to rattle as I cycled. The thread on the bolt was long, so it wasn't about to fall off, but the noise was irritating. My multitool had an Allen key on it that fitted. So I tightened it up, but it would come loose again. I needed a heavier-duty Allen key with a bit more leverage to tighten it. So I was on the lookout for a bike shop.

But for now, my mind was on getting breakfast and a caffeine refuel. So I headed off with this in mind.

Today's route headed away from any built-up areas and initially traversed Chipping Sodbury Common. Not a shop or café in sight for breakfast. Only farmhouses here by the look of it.

The Common before the Second World War was an area of bushes & trees until it was turned into farmland to grow crops for food during the war years. A golf course was built on the Common not long after, the holes fenced off to keep the cows away. People now use the Common for outdoor recreation: walking, picnics, horse-riding, and jogging.

On the Common, herds of Friesian cows were allowed to graze from June to November, wandering wherever they liked. I dodged a few who had parked themselves in the middle of the road. Then in a moment of lapsed concentration, I cycled right through a squelchy cowpat. Chef Snoopy was panicking, but he had his waterproof jacket on, so he was OK. Having seen cyclists, whose bikes don't have mudguards, with a stripe of mud up their back, I was never so pleased to have mudguards as I was on that day!

I kept cycling, the common was a big place, and I assumed that a few areas of Common land were joined together here. To avoid busy roads I headed north-east initially towards the Wiltshire border, skimmed the Cotswolds before turning west through Wickwar, and then headed north towards Gloucester.

Continuing north, passing under the M5, I was still hungry, looking for breakfast, and then came across the village of Ham. This was too much; would the next village be called Eggs?

Fortunately, shortly after Ham I cycled into the town of Berkeley and found the Perfect Blend Coffee Shop, a convenient cycle stand outside in full view from the seating inside.

'The biggest breakfast you have and a latte please' I requested.

I needed something like this every morning I thought. It proved to be a popular stop for cyclists. More riders pulled up as I was leaving.

The route was nice and flat from here, and I was back on the route suggested by the book, NCN45, running parallel with the River Severn estuary, as it joined up with the Gloucester and Sharpness Canal on its way to the centre of Gloucester.

A few cruise boats plied up and down the canal with canal-goers enjoying the trip, and the usual dog walkers along the banks provided obstacles to swerve around.

The canal had mainly swing bridges that opened to allow boats through and I passed over a few as I cycled along, the route switching from one side of the canal to the other. One bridge was curiously named Splatt bridge, raising the question of how such things got their name. Did the bridge accidentally come down on a boat? SPLATT! Who knows!

My legs were doing OK today. I must be getting used to this cycling lark. My backside was a different story. I wasn't sure at this point why I was getting so sore, but the second half of every day was getting increasingly uncomfortable.

However, I had to be thankful for small mercies. On previous long-distance cycles, I had issues with my knees. On one trip of 150 miles over three days, nearing the end, my right knee ballooned to twice its size and I could barely walk on it, on the other trip my knees started clicking and aching. Both issues were resolved by lowering my saddle height. So at least I had made it this far without such issues reoccurring.

Gloucester appeared on the horizon, much smaller than I imagined it to be. A bit like Bristol the canal took me to the quayside which had been renovated, the old and new living together in a sort of harmony. I wandered about the area but had the same problem as in Bristol. The quayside was packed with people and there was little opportunity to get food on the street.

I pushed the bike through a shopping centre, feeling very out of place, and drawing strange looks from passers-by. A touring cyclist was probably not a regular sight in most shopping centres I had to admit.

'Snoop, we didn't come on this trip to window shop. Let's get out of here'

So I pushed on and the route took me straight out of Gloucester without seeing much of the city at all; all of the city was east of the canal and River Severn, and as the route was following the river, I simply skimmed the city.

As I left, I could see the medieval Gloucester Cathedral towering over the skyline a short distance away. The viewing of its architecture, stained glass, artefacts, and the tomb of King Edward II would need to wait for another day. Further to the east of Gloucester were the main part of the famous Cotswolds 'area of natural beauty'. More places to revisit at another time perhaps.

Once clear of Gloucester the route quickly diverted onto well-tarmacked traffic-free single-track country roads still running parallel to the River Severn, through rich flat fertile land, all of which made for very pleasant cycling. Field after field went by with various crops and lots of tall fields of sweetcorn that looked ready for harvest.

Tewksbury was the next destination and as I approached a road junction, I again doubted the planned route following the National Cycle Network. A road sign pointing to the right and downhill stated 'Tewksbury 3 miles'. Great not too far. But the planned NCN route told me to go left and uphill.

I paused and absorbed the logic of this, then I checked the route on Kamoot. The NCN route went left for a short distance and then turned right to go in a big loop up a hill and back down to the main road nearer to Tewksbury. The Sustrans cycle route was 4.5 miles.

'Snoop, do you think we should rebel and just take the 3-mile downhill route?'

Chef Snoopy was a rebel at heart, so we chose to turn right down the main road, the shorter route, which wasn't busy at all and downhill all the way!

At the bottom of the hill, the road narrowed to a single track with traffic lights over Mythe Bridge, built in 1826. Unbeknown to me at the time, I was passing over the first of several bridges designed by Scottish civil engineer Thomas Telford.

My cycle stand was rattling again, so I Google bike shops and found an Autospares shop that also did bikes in Tewksbury.

'Afternoon! I'm touring and my stand keeps coming loose. Any chance I could borrow or purchase a big Allen key with good leverage?' I was hoping for the former.

The guy in the shop was really helpful. I borrowed a monster Allen key and I was able to get the leverage to tighten up the stand bolt, probably tightening it more than it had ever been tightened before.

'That should hold it. Thanks very much!'

I found a fish and chip shop in Tewksbury (Yes!) and in the absence of finding a free bench to sit on and eat, I stood outside Tewksbury Abbey and balanced my dinner on the bike saddle.

I tucked into my dinner and took in my lovely surroundings when a lady with a dog walked by and I said hello.

'There's so much litter about. Nobody has any respect anymore' she said. I wasn't sure if this was directed at me for the impending disposal of my fish & chips paper but I engaged with her.

'Is that a problem around here?' I said.

'Just look at it,' she said pointing to some papers blowing about. 'I've lived here forty years and people had more respect back then'.

I think she was having a bad day and I felt like I had to state that I would put my wrapper in the bin, but I didn't. She wandered off muttering to herself.

It would be half an hour to my destination for the day, a site which I shall call The Farm-with-No-Name, for reasons which will become apparent. So I set off knowing I didn't have far to go.

I had got into a mindset of looking forward to arriving at the campsites on my journey, as I knew that another day was under my belt, and I could relax. So I was a little concerned on arriving at The Farm-with-No-Name to what looked like a deserted farm and farmyard. If this had been mid-west America, there would have been tumbleweed blowing about.

Broken and rusty farm machinery littered the potholed yard, the place was overgrown with weeds and what looked like a large camping field was deserted apart from one small tent. Was I going to find anyone here?

'This doesn't look promising Snoop'. He looked a little worried.

There were no lights on in the farmhouse, but I knocked on the door anyway.

After a few minutes, an elderly gentleman answered.

'Hello, I called a while ago and booked a camping pitch for the night...'

He looked at me blankly, puzzled and adjusted his hearing aid. I was about to repeat myself in a slightly louder and clearer tone of voice when he turned and disappeared back into the house.

An elderly lady appeared. When I say elderly, here's me at the age of sixty, no spring chicken myself, and these people seemed a good deal older than me.

Anyway, the lady seemed to remember I had booked and she stepped out of the doorway followed by a couple of terriers that ran up to me and I patted them.

'It's £10 a night and £2 for a shower,' she said.

I handed over £12 cash and she took me over to a broken metal gate that led into the camping field.

'Pitch your tent anywhere' she stated.

It was a huge field and a solitary tent occupied a spot down one side. I headed the other way looking for a good spot, however, the field was very rough and uneven and I noticed dog mess in places. I eventually found a fairly flat clean-looking spot and pitched. I was wondering about the occupants of the other tent - there were no signs of life.

The lady retreated to the farmhouse, and I started to unpack my stuff. As I was pitching up, the terriers raced back over the field and started barking at me. Snoop was hiding in my backpack terrorised. Then they turned around and raced back to the farmhouse.

'Snoop, you're a dog are you not? It's your job to defend your owner!'

I wasn't getting a good feeling about this place!

I settled down, and it was a noisy location. Thump, thump, thump, thump. Some kind of late-night roadworks seemed to be happening locally. Along with this, it sounded like a bunch of bikers were racing their motorcycles up and down a nearby road.

A Portakabin on-site, its door unhinged, housed the toilets, a single shower, and a wash hand basin. Another Portakabin housed a small kitchen area with a table & kettle for hot water. Unfortunately, both places had been taken over by the local spider population, so I didn't bother having a shower but made my way back to the relative safety of the tent.

Still no sign of life in the mystery tent. It was a restless night, even after the road noise had died down. I didn't feel safe.

Mrs B got the lowdown on my worst campsite so far, and she expressed her concern. But I assured her that I was likely to make it through the night.

Alan Loach

Day eight - Scrapes and scrambles

Morning came, and I realised that I had been cycling for one week. But my celebration was overshadowed by the weather, which was grey and overcast, and reflected the doom and gloom mood of the campsite.

But things got worse. I was itching and had spots all over my body which looked like insect bites. Did something get into the tent last night? The ground was quite dirty, what could it be? Then it dawned on me, that I patted the farm dogs, they must have had fleas.

I quickly sprayed myself with the insect repellent that Mrs B had given me. It was perhaps a little too late to repel insects that had already bitten me, but I was hoping it would drive them off if they were still in my clothes or bedding.

A piece of advice, don't spray this stuff in an enclosed space like a tent, I burst out of the tent choking on the fumes from the spray.

'Don't worry Snoop we're getting out of here as soon as we can' He was traumatised by the dogs the previous evening and I had visions of him being torn limb from limb.

I quickly packed up my stuff, not bothering to eat anything before my departure, I was desperate to get away from this place ASAP. I didn't want to stay here a moment longer than I had to.

Making my way through the broken gate and swerving around the deep potholes on the driveway, the mystery tent remained lifeless as I made my exit.

'Perhaps that's where they put the bodies of the campers who didn't make it through the night Snoop?'

Chef Snoopy raised a questioning eyebrow. I got the message.

I continued to head north tracking the River Severn and felt the heaviness lift off me as the miles progressed.

A few miles on, I glimpsed the line of the Malvern Hills to the west and thought about when Mrs B and I had spent a week near Ledbury, west of the Malverns, just a few years ago. It took us about seven hours to drive home from here, and I was now cycling a similar journey and distance, which was going to take a little longer: seven days!

The flat countryside rolled by and after a few more miles, I crossed over the M5 and looked down to see what I was missing – miles and miles of backed-up traffic. It was moments like this that made cycling such a pleasure. No traffic queues, pushing along at your own pace with little to hold you back.

Worcester was the next big town I would pass through; the route into the city was on cycleways that ran through several housing estates to the city centre and a bridge over the Severn. Again a city much smaller than I imagined. For some reason, I imagined the capital city of Worcestershire to be a big town or city. Apparently not, being just 12 square miles in size and just over 100,000 inhabitants. Lots of history here, but again my route didn't pass by it.

I stopped at a McDonald's for breakfast and a latte, then no sooner was I going through Worcester, I was going out again into the countryside. Just 5 miles from one side of the city to the other, and in no time I was back out in the Worcestershire countryside passing vast fields of sunflowers and various other crops.

Along the way, passing over the Droitwich Canal a couple of times, it was good to see narrowboats and locks in action. I passed old barns that were preserved in this part of the country for historic interest, but in reality, looked on the verge of collapsing and maybe should have just been pulled down, and spotted a

Tudor-style building occupied by Tesco. Someone on the blog commented, 'I wonder if Will Shakespeare bought his baked beans from here?'

Stourport and Bewdley were interesting and attractive Georgian towns with the intertwining of the River Severn and the canals and much evidence of their industrial past.

In fact, in cycling over Bewdley Bridge, built in 1798, this was another Thomas Telford bridge. I read that he designed at least 40 bridges in Shropshire alone, along with numerous others up and down the country. Telford was at the cutting edge of bridge design in his time and designed several suspension bridges. So new was this technology, that it was reported that he said lengthy prayers before the chains took the weight of the bridge.

I continued north still tracking the River Severn as NCN45 made a diversion through the Wyre forest and a couple of country parks towards Bridgnorth. Lovely scenery and trails, but what was described as a cycleway in some places was stretching it a little. At the end of it all, I had cycled through undergrowth, climbed over fences, fought with nettles, and my legs were full of scratches from weeds and brambles. The worst part was that looking at the map later I could have avoided all this with a much shorter road route.

So my advice would be, don't take NCN45 north of Bewdley. Cycle the B roads. In fact, I would avoid NCN45 all the way to Ironbridge from here, as it passes along some very rough tracks.

I arrived in Bridgnorth a bit battered and bruised and refuelled at Greggs. Bridgnorth looked like a very interesting place with an interesting industrial legacy, narrow streets and very tall chimneys. The River Severn split the town into the High Town and the Low Town. If I had been bagging Thomas Telford bridges, I would have cycled over the bridge which joined the two halves, but my route followed the western bank of the Severn.

Leaving Bridgnorth, and continuing parallel with the River Severn, the route turned onto a rough compacted hardcore road. Progress was slow and I figured I might have to check the nuts and bolts on the bike after the shaking it was taking. I was back on NCN45.

Halfway along the route towards Ironbridge, I screeched to a halt. The landowner had put up signs to say the cycleway was now private access and to find a different way. My backside was sore, my legs were shredded and aching, the bike was all shaken up, and Snoop was having a nervous breakdown.

Did Sustrans know about the route closure? I stared at the sign in disbelief, then checked Komoot to see if a reroute was possible. But there was no other way apart from going 5 miles back to Bridgnorth and taking the road route to Ironbridge. A total of 15 miles.

At this point, I was only 5 miles from my destination for the day.

I stood for a while longer.

'What do we do Snoop?' It was a rhetorical question as I already knew the answer. I just needed confirmation. I was getting a bit annoyed at yet another setback today and became quite indignant.

So with Snoop in silent agreement, I decided to keep going and plead ignorance should I be stopped. I passed the sign and scoured the landscape for an irate landowner with a shotgun, or for someone in a Land Rover waiting to mow down cyclists disobeying their signage.

There were woods on either side of the path and I was expecting to cycle past a house or two. I figured if I was spotted, I could try cycling as fast as I could. On foot, they would never catch me. Or perhaps I should get off and walk as if walking would be a lesser crime than cycling.

I cycled as swiftly as I could over the rough road surface, my eyes scouring the landscape around me for movement. I had visions of a couple of Dobermans jumping out of the trees and giving chase. I needn't have been concerned as I wasn't pulled up, didn't pass any properties, and after a couple of miles, I emerged from the shaky path onto a nice smooth public road heading into Ironbridge.

I was so relieved to get to Ironbridge. The Gorge Campsite was at the top of a hill, but it was worth it, even though I pushed the bike up the last part of the hill. A lovely site compared to the previous evening.

'You've brought the sunshine'. a camper greeted me as the sun burst through the clouds. 'It's been dull and wet up to now'.

'Glad to be of service' I replied

The site was very busy, but there was plenty of space, and I pitched up on a nice spot.

'Are you here for the demolition?' the guy in the next tent asked.

'Erm, no I'm cycling to John O'Groats. What demolition?' I said.

'The old Ironbridge power station chimney is being demolished tomorrow, it's an amazing vantage point up here!' He pointed to a very tall tower a short distance away, 'The BBC are coming to film it!'

So that's why it was so busy here!

'I guess it'll be a different view tomorrow?' I commented 'I'll be away I'm afraid, but it sounds like it'll be an interesting watch'.

I settled down, tending my shredded legs and the insect bites. Glad I brought along some Germolene.

My body was getting used to the daily aches and pains, which freed up my mind for other things. I had been away from home and Mrs B for over a week, and I wished she was with me to experience this amazing journey. However, this would have been her worst nightmare.

To start with, Mrs B had balance problems with bikes, and although she tried very hard she didn't enjoy cycling or feel safe on a bike. She was OK riding in a straight line but couldn't turn corners - her own admission! It was true. A sudden change of direction and she went one way and the bike went another - she was over the handlebars!

She tried so hard to get the hang of riding a bike, but the final straw for her was a cycle along the Forth & Clyde Canal towpath. A great path for the likes of Mrs B; flat, quite straight and with no obstructions apart from the occasional dog walker.

We were cycling along in line quite happily with Mrs B behind when a cyclist approached from the other direction. I put the brakes on to slow down and pass on the narrow path, but she hadn't noticed and swerved to avoid a collision, ending up in the canal. It took three of us to drag her out. She was a little shocked, to say the least, and that was the last time she was on her bike.

LEJOG would have been a nightmare for Mrs B, but it was a dream come true for me. So in doing LEJOG, I would be doing it without her, and I felt pangs of selfishness and the need for her approval.

One day we were both sitting watching the TV, which was not remotely cycling-related and LEJOG popped into my head once more. I blurted out 'What would you think about me cycling from Land's End to John O'Groats?....'

Her answer was crucial. I didn't want to spend too much money on doing this cycle as it would mean we may not be able to afford to go on a 'proper' holiday because I'd spent all our disposable income on LEJOG. Not that any of our income could be regarded as disposable. Having been brought up to make every penny count, I was by default looking for the most economical way to do this trip anyway.

Camping seemed like the best option, but Mrs B didn't do camping, – she might have been swayed by glamping at a push, but camping no way, and certainly not the kind of camping I had in mind. She understandably liked her comforts. Even going away for one night she would pack a huge case with items for any and every eventuality. We could have done B&Bs, but three or four weeks of B&Bs worked out at quite an outlay in accommodation costs alone. This could have been the cost of flights and accommodation to Spain or the Canaries for a couple of weeks. Mrs B would have preferred this.

So to this end, I was thinking I could just do the trip myself, get it over and done with to stop it niggling at the back of my mind, and when possible we could both go on a nice holiday somewhere warm.

But I needed her approval. Would she think it was just another one of my hare-brained ideas?

She answered my question, 'You can do it yourself'. That's what I liked about Mrs B. No-nonsense, straight to the point, she spoke her mind honestly. It was what I was hoping to hear, and after making sure she would be OK with me being away for so long, I knew I had to go for it.

So here I was fulfilling my dream. She wasn't with me in person, and I was missing her, but she was always there at the end of the phone.

I settled down in my tent and called her at home to yet again recount today's sorry tale of my injuries and struggles. If she were here in person she would be armed with plasters and paracetamol, but I had to cope with all this myself today.

'Let me put some New Skin on it', she would say. This was her favourite fix for almost anything.

My usual reaction would be 'But I like to let air get to it'

New Skin was a thick gluey liquid, sold in a small bottle with an applicator. It could be painted onto minor cuts and grazes, and when dry after a few minutes, it provided a barrier to dirt and germs. I often succumbed to her request, but I still believed that sometimes good old fresh air was the best.

By this time, the sun was going down for the last time on the Ironbridge Power Station chimney, and it was receding into the darkness of the countryside in which it stood. I couldn't help feeling a tinge of sadness for this tall inanimate object, which surprised me.

Snoop gave me a look as if I was a little unhinged. What was this cycle doing to me?

I fell asleep and dreamed of a giant Jelly Baby clinging to the top of the power station chimney. He was roaring like King Kong and lashing out at the circling helicopters, as the explosions detonated at the base, bringing the structure crashing to the ground.

Day nine - Nettle Bashing

Demolition day 7.45am and the campsite was starting to buzz. The 204-metre chimney was due to come down between 10am and 1pm, weather conditions permitting. The weather was calm despite a damp mist, so it looked promising. But Snoop and I had to leave and head for Manchester.

'Snoop, I know you would have liked to see this chimney being blown up, but we have to go'. He went in a huff and didn't speak to me for the rest of the day.

There was no way we could hang about until 10am. I just hoped that the mist lifted so the campers would have a good view.

I had a long day planned today, 83 miles. This was by design.

Tonight, I would be sleeping in luxury. I had booked a night at the Premier Inn in Sale, Manchester, as I figured that at this stage I would need a good clean-up. I didn't have to arrive before dark to put the tent up so the longer distance wasn't too much of an issue.

In planning, the route for today seemed relatively flat with more downs than ups, even though the elevations totalled 2300ft. I was telling myself I should be able to make good time, but I'd made this mistake before. Anyway, I'd planned what I'd planned so I just had to accept it and get on with it.

Leaving the campsite and heading downhill, I came out of the mist, and the day was overcast but calm.

Heading past Ironbridge Gorge Museum, the area was filled with industrial history, an impressive railway viaduct, mine buildings and miners' housing. All renovated and despite their humble origins, now probably highly sought-after accommodation.

The cycle track out of Ironbridge followed what was presumably an old mine railway. I was heading for Telford and was determined to find a latte somewhere. My morning latte was becoming an essential boost for me.

Telford wasn't too far away and I sensed a familiarity about it. The town centre in particular had a utilitarian feel, with very square functional buildings, underpasses, overpasses and lots of concrete. It wouldn't be until I looked up its history that I found out it was a 1960s New Town, similar in many ways to Cumbernauld in Scotland.

After passing through the town centre, on the outskirts was a large Asda store with an instore Costa. Perfect! I looked around for somewhere to lock up the bike and an Asda trolley guy must have seen me looking.

'The bike rack's over there mate' he pointed me to the back of a trolley shelter.

I locked up the bike, as usual, a bit wary of who might be around should I leave it, but the bike racks were directly opposite a Timpson portacabin in the car park and I figured it would be OK for a few minutes. I emerged with food supplies, a large vanilla latte and a breakfast roll with sausage and tomato sauce.

'Where are youse heading mate?' the trolley guy reappeared. He had a most appealing West Midland accent.

'Oh morning! I'm staying in Manchester tonight'

'Oh my God! Oh my God!' He exclaimed rather exuberantly. 'That's quite a journey', and he was right I had almost 80 miles to go.

I said I was heading eventually to John O'Groats, and he could hardly contain himself. I got three 'Oh my God's for that revelation. I felt like saying yes God is going with me so I would be OK.

He told me he went cycling with his boy at the weekends and thought he was doing well at 10 miles.

'It's not the distance, it's just getting out there that matters,' I told him.

My parents both came from the Midlands and I guess I have a soft spot for the accent because of them. However mum was a bit more Lancashire which was where she was born. It's a strange thing, but you never think of your parents as having an accent. I guess you hear them from the moment you're born and it's just the way they speak.

I think the only time I noticed that they had an accent was when their voice was recorded, perhaps on a voicemail message or in a video.

I always remember that Mum had a telephone voice. She would answer the phone for the hotel and would sound frightfully posh.

She recounted to us a story of when they first had a boarding house in Blackpool in the 1950s or 1960s. This was in the days when people would post handwritten letters to book a holiday in a guest house.

One day a booking letter came in for a man called Mr Onions and there was a great debate in the family about how Mr Onions pronounced his surname. Mum figured it would be pronounced *Oh-nie-ons*, with the accent on the middle syllable as it sounded a bit posher.

The time of arrival came and the Onions family checked in.

'Hello, Mr Oh-nie-ons' Mum said in greeting

'It's just pronounced Onions thank you!' was the reply!

Leaving Telford, I headed on NCN55 for the market town of Newport, quite a contrast from Telford, where many of the buildings were of red brick construction, and some Tudor style whitewashed with black wood facades. Not to be confused with Newport in Wales. The main street was said to be of Norman design and distinctively long and wide. It certainly had a very old English market town appearance.

Yarn-bombing seemed to be the thing around here. Knitted coats for lampposts, bollards, post-boxes, and other items of street furniture. Some were very clever and must have taken ages to knit.

NCN552 then led me through to Market Drayton on single-track and farm roads. It was early September and bumper crops were growing in the passing fields. In some, tractors ran back and forth, and other farm machinery worked on the crops.

I passed through Norton in Hales, which had a very Miss Marple murder mystery feel to it. A quaint old English village. What was lurking behind those ornate doorways? From here I left Shropshire and entered Cheshire.

The route to Manchester was quite flat, passing through Nantwich, known for an annual International Cheese Show and a Food Festival. Winsford, home of the UK's largest rock salt (halite) mine and Northwich, also famed for its salt pans which had been around since Roman times. Lovely countryside mixed with lots of history.

With the mileage I had to cover today, I wasn't able to stop and explore. I pushed on, not stopping to take in many sights or take many photos. The route was heading directly north to meet up with NCN62 which would take me directly to my destination for tonight.

The final stretch before Sale was through a wooded area with narrow paths. Again the paths weren't well maintained and nettles and brambles completely covered the route in places.

Chef Snoopy covered his eyes as we ploughed through the vegetation at speed. My legs were taking a punishment again. But as I was moving at quite a good pace I made an interesting discovery - if you hit a nettle hard enough it doesn't (or maybe can't) sting you. I've got you sussed now Mr or Mrs nettle! I just need to cycle a bit faster when I see you...

It was 7.30pm and starting to get dark and I was hoping that my destination was close, although I did have bike lights in my rucksack.

Then all of a sudden I burst out of the woodland and there I was at the Premier Inn. I let out a sigh of relief, a warm comfy bed awaited me and I would eat hot food at the Brewers Fayre next door!

It had been a long day today, 83 miles and almost 12 hours out and about between taking wrong turns, blog stops, breaks and stopping to eat & drink. But the reward was a night in a proper bed.

At the reception, I went to check-in.

'Evening,' I said to the receptionist, 'We, I mean I, have a room booked for the night' I looked at Snoop not wanting to offend him as I'd only booked the room for myself. He winked at me and I knew what he wanted me to ask...

'Is it possible to have a ground floor room?' I wasn't holding out much hope, but I thought it was worth asking.

'I'm afraid you need to specify that when you book,' the receptionist said, as she looked up my booking on her computer, '...but it looks like you're on the ground floor anyway!' I think Snoop must have given her 'the look'.

'You're fortunate, we have a big party of cyclists booked in and they're all upstairs'. Little did she know, I had someone looking after me.

I arrived in my room, and it was luxurious compared to where I'd been in recent weeks. I quickly changed and headed for food next door. I ate well, with fish & chips at the Brewers Fayre, 'Table for one please!', but I missed the company of Mrs B. Not that Snoop wasn't good company, but he was the strong silent type.

Simple food but delicious. But strangely enough, I missed sitting cross-legged in my tent, in the peace and quiet with the tent flap open, looking out to the countryside and opening a tin of beans.

Back in my room, I was particularly grateful for the bath. It soothed my injuries, aches, and pains, and I soaked in it until I was extremely wrinkly. I scrubbed up well and even shaved. Although 10 days of stubble growth, which was now becoming grey in places, didn't amount to much.

I plugged in all my devices for a complete recharge and reflected on the journey so far.

It's said that most cyclists take ten to fourteen days to cover the typical LEJOG road route of about 870 to 900 miles. The Sustrans route was longer and as said before, I knew this. But I wasn't prepared for the poor quality of some of the 'cycleways'. However, I was generally pleased that the route was fairly traffic-free.

The road route seemed a bit dangerous - I'd had a few close calls on my cycling commute in the past, and I was doing this to enjoy it. I didn't need the stress of sharing the road with juggernauts. I had been grumbling to myself about the Sustrans route in the book, and some of the chosen paths justified this. But having seen the quantity of traffic on the main roads when I had crossed or encountered them, I was thankful for the quiet back roads.

However, some of the routes so far I would have rerouted had I known a better way. Hindsight is a great thing.

My biggest issue at this point was a very sore backside. I hadn't been saddle sore since I first started cycling 13 years previously, so what was going on?

During planning this trip I thought about what I should wear. Up to that point, I had just worn bog-standard mountain bike style, baggy shorts with no padding. I think my backside had toughened up over the years, and

I never got saddle sore. I even did the Sustrans Coast to Coast from Whitehaven to Newcastle with no padding and my backside was just fine! But LEJOG was much further so I thought I might give 'proper' cycle shorts a try. After all, the stretchiness meant they moved with you and fitted neatly, there was no bagginess to flap about causing wind resistance and friction. Plus they had the added 'benefit' of some extra padding. It all made sense. I purchased 2 different pairs.

Well in hindsight, I can say that padded cycle shorts don't work for me. I think there must be something odd about my backside because the padding seemed to dig in after a few miles and the shorts became so uncomfortable.

I spent a while in the Premiere Inn trying to unpick the stitching that held the padding on, but it was triple-stitched, I didn't have the right tools, and I just wasn't getting anywhere. Mrs B was the expert at this kind of thing, so I would just have to persevere until I got home.

I did consider a couple of temporary solutions. The first was, 'Perhaps I could wear them back to front?' This was only a fleeting consideration as the padding would be at the front. A look that might have drawn more than a few sniggers from passers-by. The second was cycling in my stripy underpants. I think this may have been more comfortable, and would probably have worked, but I didn't want to be trending on social media for my fashion sense.

I would eventually discover that the padding on one of the pairs of shorts was slightly off-centre and they never sat correctly on the saddle. And here was me thinking I had a squinty backside. Anyway, my backside wasn't having any of it, to the extent that even the non-squinty pair of shorts were uncomfortable.

After reporting into Mrs B, saying goodnight to Snoop, and thanking my bike for getting me this far, I collapsed into my big fluffy king-sized bed and was out like a light.

Miles of Memories

Day ten - Fine Dining in the Forest

I woke and panicked…

'Where am I, Snoop where are we?'

We were of course still in the Premier Inn, but the room was pitch black with very effective blackout curtains.

I got a good, if a little too warm, sleep, and found myself longing to be back in my tent. I was getting very used to the simplicity of popping it up and crawling inside. I had everything I needed in all my bags. Indeed the choice of kit was proving to be good so far, the lightweight two-man Coleman Darwin tent was spacious, and the extra space inside was useful for storing the panniers and bags overnight. My down-filled sleeping bag, blow-up sleeping mat and blow-up pillow were so cosy. But the best thing was waking up with the fresh cool air on my face, the sound of the wildlife, the wind in the trees and the glow of the sunrise on the tent. Waking up was such a joy, and if I didn't have places to get to before the end of the day, I could have lain there breathing in the peace and tranquillity for quite some time.

The hotel room, as nice and as comfortable as it was, wasn't quite the same.

'Well Snoop, at least today we'll get a good breakfast to start the day'

At the Brewers Fayre, next door, we had the all-you-can-eat breakfast and a latte. So I ate all I could eat and then some more and figured this would sustain me for a good part of the day. I felt refreshed and ready to roll. Less achy than I expected to be from the previous day's distance.

My scars and insect bite were receding now, not only physically but in my memory too. Over the years of cycling, I had become accustomed to my legs taking a bit of a battering. The worst time was when I had a pair of lightweight alloy pedals. I seemed to be unable to avoid hitting my legs off the sharp metal of the pedals, either when dismounting, picking up the bike to store it or getting through narrow gaps, my legs got in the way and ended up all cut, battered and bruised.

But there was one thing I noticed: the more I cycled the quicker my legs healed. It seemed to be a fact. It's said that regular exercise may speed up the wound-healing process by as much as 25%. Exercise draws oxygen to the wounds and helps the healing process, boosts the immune function, and produces anti-inflammatory agents that signalled the body to build and repair tissue.

As I left the Premier Inn, with my nice smooth plastic-pedalled bike, some of the cycling group were negotiating the stairs with their bikes, and others were congregating outside. They had two backup vans probably carrying everything they needed to keep them in their saddles no matter what, and bikes and gear you would likely need a mortgage to afford. Some 'plain clothes' guys were buzzing about with pumps and tools. The whole setup seemed to say they were some kind of cycling elite or professional club.

'Where are you all off to today?' I asked a girl in pink Lycra. I think I must have interrupted her train of thought.

'What?' she said. I rephrased

'Looks like you're all set to go, where are you heading?'. She didn't seem to want to engage in any conversation,

'South' she said and turned away.

I looked over at Chef Snoopy and he looked at me. He seemed to shrug his shoulders without moving. I don't know how he did it.

Greater Manchester beckoned and very soon I would be in my home county: Lancashire. I say home county, meaning where I was born rather than where I now live.

Starting on NCN62 then on NCN6, I would be heading mostly north again today to end up on the edge of the Forest of Bowland north of Clitheroe.

My route soon took me to the banks of the River Mersey, upstream from Liverpool, which I followed for a few miles. Then branching away from the River I traversed several bridges and underpasses towards Manchester city centre. It was a typical cityscape and urban sprawl, with buses & trams, graffiti & posters, canals & rivers, old industry & new technology side by side. But the cycle availability of cycleways was very good.

Despite the good cycleways, it was still a challenge negotiating the streets of the city centre. Komoot was not being very helpful and I ended up off course several times, going around in circles at one point, even though my sense of direction is normally pretty good.

 I was also looking for somewhere to stock up on food. A small local shop where I could keep the bike in view, but like I mentioned before the NCN routes tended to take you down all the back streets, through parks and along canal paths, as they're quieter, and I didn't spot any local shops.

Now Manchester is famous for a few things and one of those things is rain. Although it was dry as I cycled through the city there was a strange sense of dampness about the place. I was beginning to realise that I was not a big fan of cities and large towns. Bristol, Gloucester, Worcester, now Manchester. I'm sure there are lovely areas in all these places, but my route didn't go near them, and I was so pleased to be out of them and back onto country roads.

I was getting a little frustrated with my slow progress in Manchester. The good provision of cycleways in the city proved to be a disadvantage, as there were too many routes to choose from and therefore taking the wrong one was quite easy. I was so glad to get through to the other side.

Continuing north after leaving the city, I joined up with the Manchester, Bury and Bolton Canal from Radcliffe to Bury. Then started heading uphill.

In a few miles, I would pass my halfway point for the whole cycle – a milestone and a photo opportunity! I stopped at Nuttall Park just before Ramsbottom.

'Say cheese Snoop!', We posed on a bench with a celebratory tin of Heinz Beans, and I posted this on the Polarsteps blog,

My total mileage so far was 576 miles. On the most direct cyclable route, according to Komoot, this could have seen me cover the whole length of England from Land's End to Gretna just over the Scottish border. But I was happy with what I'd done so far despite the hills, scratches & scrapes, detours, rough paths, and going around in circles.

Setting off for the second half of LEJOG, we passed through Ramsbottom. Now there's a name for a town. I looked it up and it had nothing to do with the backsides of male sheep, but likely came from the Olde English word 'hramsa' meaning garlic and 'bopm' which referred to land at the bottom of a valley suitable for agriculture. So presumably 'Garlic Valley'. Arguably better than Ramsbottom, but the jury may be out on that one.

Shortly I passed through the small hamlet of Irwell Vale and encountered possibly the worst cycle path of the whole trip. The surface was what appeared to be made of discarded bricks, and being on an uphill section, completely un-cyclable. Snoop looked at me as if to say,

'You're not going to cycle over that are you?'

I don't think I could have done if I had tried, so getting off and pushing was the only option. I found out later that this section had been bypassed, but NCN6 hadn't been updated on the maps.

I continued on a largely uphill trajectory through the north-western industrial landscape, its manufacturing and mining past was much in evidence here, mills and quarries, abandoned and repurposed.

The route rose to almost 1000 ft at Rising Bridge before dropping down again to Accrington. From here, we joined up with the Leeds and Liverpool Canal as it crossed the M65 and skirted Rishton. A town famous apparently for its cricket team. As I hadn't a clue about cricket I was not the wiser.

NCN6 continued from Rishton westwards to Blackburn, but I took a right turn and headed uphill, continuing on my northerly trajectory, to NCN90.

The road rose again steeply just before the town of Whalley, but despite the climbs, I wasn't getting off and pushing now! The views back over my route, now hill farm country, highlighted just how far I had come today after rising from the industrial landscape. I was 45 miles in and had 15 miles to go.

Whalley Old Road provided an exhilarating ride down from almost 1000ft to 300 ft in 3 miles. On the way down I spotted the famous Whalley Viaduct built between 1846 and 1850, known locally as the Whalley Arches. This was a railway bridge of 48 spans at almost 2000 feet long that crossed the River Calder.

And there it was, the answer to one of life's most important questions; 'Where's Wally?'. It was right here, and I cycled into it.

The town of Whalley seemed like a very nice place, and I probably should have stopped at a shop for some supplies. I cycled past a few, not realising that this would be the last town of any size where I'd find a shop. I would regret this later.

The road now wasn't too hilly and I was on a clockwise circuit of Clitheroe to get to my destination. It was only sixty miles today, but my backside wasn't happy and once again I was relieved to arrive at the campsite.

The habit I'd got into of pushing on and not stopping much wasn't doing me much good. Today's push was to make up the time I had wasted picking my way through Manchester. But in reality, I arrived at the campsite at 5.30pm so I could have, and should have, stopped more often.

Dobbies Farm campsite was a sight for sore legs. The site was on the edge of the Forest of Bowland and the countryside was amazing, rolling countryside, leading to rolling hills. I rolled into the site and met up with the site manager Karen.

I had been communicating with Karen via email several weeks earlier after spotting the site online. Their website stated, '2 persons and a tent £18', so before booking, I emailed a question:

'Do you have a rate for one person and a tent?'.

The reply was 'It will probably be £18 since our showers are now free to use'.

I didn't get the logic of this but booked the site anyway. On arrival I thought I might ask about charging up my devices, hoping she might throw in an electric hookup as the pitch was a little expensive.

'If you're only charging up your phones, and you don't have an electric heater in those bags' she glanced at my bags, 'I can hook you up for an extra £2'.

I felt like saying it was a Mary Poppins bag and I had a couple of standard lamps in there along with the electric heater, but I thought that might not go down well. So I took her up on her offer and handed over £20.

It was true that I had my devices all charged up the night before but being four nights from home and moving into more remote areas, I wasn't sure when I would next be able to charge them up.

I pitched and realised I was hungry. The site was quite remote with no local shops open after 6pm and it was 6 miles to Clitheroe, the nearest town of any size.

'Do any food takeaway shops deliver to the site?' I asked Karen, hoping for those magic words, 'Dominos deliver'....

'No one delivers up here,' she said, 'But the Coach & Horses in the village do food. It's a ten-minute walk'. This sounded good, country pub food.

I reviewed my stock of food. I had two bananas and two bags of Jelly Babies, so the Coach & Horses sounded like a good idea. As it was Saturday night, I called the pub and booked a table in case they were busy. I quickly got changed and made my way down to the village.

As I walked I realised that I was really hungry and could eat a horse. So unless they had more than two horses they might need to rename the pub to the Coach and Horse!

Walking through the door it looked like a typical country pub, the bar was to the right and the dining area to the left. It looked a little posh, and I hoped that my blue skip hat, burnt orange quilted jacket, burgundy chinos and bright yellow trainers wouldn't see me being turned away. Fortunately, I must have passed the dress code check and was seated in a nice corner of the bar. I ordered a pint of Coke. I was having visions of a nice big fillet of fish, in some tasty batter, a squeeze of lemon, with a nice pile of chunky chips and some mushy peas, or perhaps a good-sized portion of homemade steak pie, with some seasonal vegetables, and perhaps some creamy mash...

The bartender brought over the à la carte menu.

'Do you do a bar meal menu?' I asked.

'This is our only menu sir...'

I scanned the menu and it was a little limited and a bit pricey. My heart sank, this was a bit more refined than I was expecting, and I was getting a bit concerned about the quantity of food that might arrive.

What to do? What were my options? I'd left Chef Snoopy guarding the tent, so I couldn't ask his advice. Should I think of an excuse and politely apologise that I had to go?

'Sorry I've got to go; I just received some bad news about my pet goldfish...'

My options were: just eat my two bananas and have Jelly Babies for breakfast. I could just starve, or I could stay and eat...

I decided to stay and order some food. I had monkfish, mash, green beans, and sweetcorn. (The actual description on the menu was of course much more appealing than this). I have to say that the food was very nice, however, the portions were probably a quarter of what I needed. I ordered a dessert of treacle tart, which was also nice.

The bartender came over when I had finished 'Was everything OK for you sir?'. I had to stop myself from saying,

'Lovely, but I've just cycled sixty miles. Could I have the whole meal again'?

But instead, I said

'It was very nice, thank you!'

Very British. I was reminded of an episode of Fawlty Towers: Two little elderly ladies had suffered appalling service in the hotel restaurant, and Basil Fawlty asked them if everything was OK. 'Lovely thank you' was the reply.

On reflection, I perhaps should have swallowed my pride and honestly admitted my situation. How could they have known? They may have taken pity on me (not that I would seek pity) and sent me away with a large take-away portion of fries.

Anyway, I made my way back to the campsite. Chef Snoopy had no sympathy for me, so I called Mrs B and offloaded my woes yet again.

Tomorrow would be Sunday, which concerned me. Shops and cafes normally open later on a Sunday, especially in the countryside. I turned to Mr Google, who confirmed my fears. No local shops would be open first thing in the morning, and the nearest place for a coffee was Ingleton twenty miles away on the other side of the Forest of Bowland. To get there my route would rise to over 1500ft.

I was going to need those bananas and Jelly Babies, as this was going to be my biggest challenge yet!

I nodded off with my stomach rumbling and dreamed of giant Jelly Babies chasing me along the road.

'Eat me, Alan...' they roared.

Miles of Memories

Alan Loach

Day eleven - The Hills... The Hills...

I woke up in the morning to gorgeous countryside and calm peaceful weather. A hazy sun was rising over the forests, pockets of mist lingered in the valley, but there wasn't a cloud in the sky. The sense of calm, stillness and peace was tangible.

I had both bananas for breakfast, had topped up the power in all my devices and was ready to head off into the hills. A couple of big hill climbs now as I headed towards the Pennines, and I felt a feeling of dread at the prospect. I needed to change my attitude. Positive thinking, that's what I needed. So I decided to tell myself that 'the hills were my friends'.

'Snoop, the hills are my friends, just so you know...'. I reaffirmed. He looked at me suspiciously. 'No offence of course. You're still my best buddy on this trip'. The reassurance was an obvious afterthought and probably didn't go down well.

As I was emptying my rubbish into the bins another camper with a bike appeared. She looked 30-something age-wise, and her bike was loaded with panniers back and front

'Hi, there! Where are you off to today?' I asked.

'Heading north'.

'Ah, me too' I replied.

I could sense she was being quite cautious with her answer, understandable, a young girl cycling by herself.

'I'm heading to John O'Groats' I announced.

'So am I,' she said,

I noticed that she had very muscly legs, so a seasoned tourer by the look of her. Chef Snoopy gave me a warning glance, but I ignored him. 'Snoop it was just an observation!'

'How far are you heading today?' I enquired.

'Oh, I just cycle and stop when and where I want. I'm doing around 100km a day. Maybe I'll bump into you along the way'

I got the message that she didn't want company, and that suited me too. Although I normally enjoy cycling with other people, because of the tight schedule I had created for myself, cycling with a buddy at this stage wasn't on my agenda. I didn't need someone to either keep up with or slow down for. Apart from that, Chef Snoopy was my co-rider, and I don't think he would have been pleased to have competition for his attention.

I headed off first at 7.30am just after our conversation and she went off to finish whatever she was doing. I assumed she would be taking the same route, as there were only a couple of route choices through the Forest of Bowland, and I was taking the most obvious. With her looking a bit fitter than me, I wondered if she might catch up with me.

I cycled up into the hills and the ascent was gradual but increasing, with a few flat stretches and valleys. The area on the map was designated an AONB, Area of Outstanding Natural Beauty, 312 square miles of rural Lancashire and part of Yorkshire, and it was indeed lovely. Initially, I cycled through the lowlands which were crisscrossed with dry stone walls. I passed picturesque farms and villages, some apparently dating from pre-historic times. Then, I climbed up higher to the dramatic open peat moorland, gritstone fells and deep valleys.

The hills were nothing like those in Cornwall, and I repeated my new phrase out loud to keep myself going.

'The hills are my friends. Yes, the hills are indeed my friends, Hello hills, I'm so glad we are friends'. Snoop visibly cringed on my behalf.

However, even with self-motivation, I ran out of energy after a while. I had after all been on the brink of starvation the night before and had a meal fit for a mouse. This morning was a Sunday, no local shops were open to buy a coffee or food. I had to make do with my meagre rations. My legs simply stopped working on one of the longer inclines and I got off to push the bike. It was at this point that Campsite Girl appeared.

'It's OK to get off and push', I told myself as she approached, trying to sound convincing in my head. 'Snoop, it's OK to get off and push'. I stopped and reached for my bag of Jelly Babies as she passed.

'Would you like a Jelly Baby' I offered, feeling a pang of embarrassment.

'No thanks' as she slowly passed me, not stopping, legs spinning like crazy.

Her bike, it seemed, was lower geared than mine. I can do a slow uphill too, but it gets to a point where you need to maintain a certain leg rotation to be able to keep going. A bit like a car trying to pull up a very steep hill in second or third gear, I just stalled. It's called cadence in cycling terms, a certain revolution-per-minute you could say. If my legs could have spun that fast I wouldn't have needed to get off and push.

'No Snoop it's not an excuse'.

It was true I was trying to justify myself, but there was some truth in the gearing.

'She's ahead of me now, I'll likely never see her again,' I thought with a guilty sense of antisocial relief.

The road dipped into a valley and through the charming village of Slaidburn, on the banks of the River Hodder, with its sandstone brick houses, dry stone walls and greener-than-green fields. It was still Sunday and still early, so again no shops for a caffeine refuel or anything else. I pressed on knowing that Ingleton was my only hope (Where's Obi-Wan Kenobi when you need him?)

The road climbed again to the 1500ft summit and I knew that after this peak there was a good downhill towards Ingleton. As I reached the crest before the downhill, I spotted a bike abandoned by the roadside.

I stopped for a second and the owner appeared from behind a dry-stone wall. It was Campsite Girl again. Snoop averted his eyes.

'Oh, hello again' she said in a slightly embarrassed tone of voice.

I was probably the last person she wanted to see. Was I going to keep bumping into her every day? We chatted briefly and I found out she was using a Garmin to plot her route, and she did have a plan after all, despite her earlier comments.

Anyway, I headed off again ahead of her. I knew at the bottom of the hill that I had planned a diversion that she most likely wasn't going to take, but even with this, I went like the clappers so that she wasn't going to overtake me yet again.

NCN90 over the Forest of Bowland joined with the westbound NCN69. This was the suggested Sustrans route. However, I intended to head the other way on the eastbound 69, and then make my own way by cutting north to Ingleton to join up with NCN68, The Pennine Cycleway. This long-distance route followed the backbone of the Pennines, so I would be in for some spectacular scenery. I would briefly travel through North Yorkshire today and then cross into Cumbria for the rest of my journey to the Scottish border.

When planning this section I had a dilemma. Following the Sustrans book, today's route was approaching 70 miles taking a loop west almost to the coast before returning east. So I figure cutting off the corner and going almost directly north might work. However, going off the designated cycle route had its risks. Even B-roads and remote-looking farm roads can be busy with cars and sometimes dangerous to cycle with all their twists, turns and potentially blind summits and corners. To try and get a feel for the roads I would view them in Google Streetview, looking at how many cars were on the road, and the type of road. This didn't always work, but generally, if the road was singletrack it was a good sign, whereas a wider road with well-defined road markings usually meant a much faster road, often with faster cars.

The diversion I planned cut off over ten miles, and although it was a little hillier, I figured that it would be less time in the saddle for my backside.

My diversion east then north seemed to work out well and I arrived in Ingleton at about 11am. I stocked up with things to eat and found a place to buy food and a latte. Campsite Girl didn't make an appearance and was likely to have gone in the opposite direction, as I thought.

Ingleton itself was a very picturesque place teeming with cyclists and people on Sunday outings.

A listed Victorian railway viaduct dominated the town, disused and unfortunately closed to the public. It spanned the valley and would have made a wonderful cycle or walkway. The sun had come out now and I sat on a bench with my latte and a chicken mayo sandwich as an early lunch.

'Snoop, this is wonderful' The warmth of the sun felt good as I relaxed on the bench and watched the world go by. I started daydreaming of a simpler life, of not going back to work but spending a life on the road with Mrs B. We would travel from place to place in a camper van without a care in the world and the sun would shine every day………….

I must have been grinning from ear to ear, Snoop was looking at me as if I'd gone off my rocker.

'You have to dream Snoop - nothing is impossible'

I headed off again, continuing northwards on NCN68 into the North Yorkshire Dales Park on single-track roads lined with traditional dry-stone walls. The valley I was cycling through was spectacular, the hills on either side covered by limestone cliffs and ridges.

I stopped along the way where several cars were parked in a layby and walkers were heading off across the valley. This was my thing, walking in the fresh air, exploring somewhere new. Sunday walkers I guess, making the most of the sunny weather.

The attraction it seemed was the popular Thornton Force waterfall. Dropping 46ft over a limestone cliff, and a stunning sight when it came into view. It wasn't visible from where I was, but I wanted to join them and study the amazing geology I was seeing, but I had to keep moving – quite a few more miles to go today.

Further along, I passed one of the entrances to Yordas Cave, a natural local curiosity, and I believe a good cave for those unfamiliar with caving. Again, there was nothing much to see from the road, (perhaps obviously), as the attraction was underground, but a huge chamber lay not far inside the entrance.

It was a popular destination for cavers, walkers, and outdoor activity groups. I must admit not being a big fan of caving, not that I've tried it, but the idea of squeezing through narrow gaps in the pitch black doesn't appeal. Perhaps something like this cave might have been OK with the gaps and caverns being reportedly bigger than normal. Maybe one day!

At the head of the valley, the road rose to almost two thousand feet, but the inclines were not too steep to get there. Only on one section did I have to get off and push, and the top of the pass gave a wonderful view of the downhill I was about to experience.

'Hold onto your hat Snoop, this is going to be good!'

The downhill dropped one thousand feet in just one mile, but then continued another three miles at a lesser gradient to the valley floor. I set off to enjoy my four miles of downhill freewheeling and started to pick up speed on the first section. It was like riding a rollercoaster but without the steep uphill parts or the loops. The downhill was exhilarating, much steeper than the uphill I had just climbed. I was thankful that I didn't have to cycle up this side of the hill.

Then just before the steep mile section ended, a sharp bend in the road appeared and a closed gate blocked the road. I screeched to a halt. Thankfully, my bike had decent brakes otherwise I wouldn't have been unable to pull up in time and might have been catapulted over the gate without the bike.

This was my first bike with disc brakes, which work in a very similar way to brakes work on a car. Traditional bike brakes have pads on the rim of the wheel which are pretty efficient. However, should the rims get dirty with mud or salt from the road, when the brakes are applied this dirt can act like sandpaper that eventually wears the rim through. The rim can then crack or snap very suddenly with the wheel jamming solid on the brake blocks. I had this happen to me twice but fortunately, both times I wasn't cycling very fast, otherwise, I could easily have been thrown off the bike.

'Please shut the gate' was the request on the sign. I obliged after going through and I was on my way again.

I descended into Dentdale, which seemed to sit within the boundaries of both Cumbria and the Yorkshire Dales. I always thought that the two were separate areas, but apparently not, they overlap. Dentdale, described as the finest of the Cumbrian Dales, was reminiscent of the landscape of the Lake District but without any lakes. White-washed stone cottages and dry-stone walls, sheep farms and cattle grids.

I stopped briefly for a snack and heard grunting and snorting. Looking over a wall I found two pigs, and they rushed up to me at the farm gate. Snoop got a real fright and pretended he hadn't seen them, but they were very friendly, much like dogs welcoming their owner. I patted them through the gate and they lay back down in the sun after a couple of minutes.

The village of Dent proved to be a total surprise; I felt like I had stepped back in time with its narrow-cobbled streets, a village cross and the George & Dragon pub bustling with customers at 2pm. I half expected a horse and cart to come charging around the corner, and a town crier clanging his bell shouting 'Oh yay!, Oh yay!, Oh yay! (or Oyez!, Oyez! Oyez! as I've seen it written). What that meant I was never quite sure. It was certainly a place with oodles of history, and extremely popular with tourists and walkers. Stopping at Dent Heritage Centre was a temptation, but I decided to keep moving.

I cycled on and through the town of Sedburgh, the last town of any size before my destination for the day. Like the previous day, I should have stopped but didn't. Planned stops just added more time to my day and I didn't really have time to delay, so I just pushed on.

The remaining miles of my route followed lots of singletrack roads, lovely quiet roads meandering in and out, up and down the Cumbrian countryside, tracking the River Lune and the M6 motorway up to Tebay.

NCN68 converged with NCN70 ten miles east of Kendal. This was where my modified route rejoined the route in the book. I was so glad I had done the reroute. This had been a good day.

Most people know Tebay from the motorway services of the same name. Independent service stations on the M6 motorway which gave a refreshing change from the same old big-chain services offerings on many motorways. There are service roads into such services, and I thought of stopping off here but decided against it as I had a Zoom meeting with friends planned so needed to get to the campsite and settle down.

My destination was just beyond Orton, and I pulled into New House Farm to be greeted by the owner with a lovely Lancashire accent. 'Ow do love, good to see yer. Av yer come far today?'

I mentioned that I'd cycled from the Clitheroe area

'By gum Love, yer must be jiggered!'.

I was indeed jiggered. I gave her my £10 for the night and she showed me to an empty field. Unlike the empty field from a few nights ago, this was a nice field bounded by dry stone walls, with picnic benches and a small toilet block in one corner.

I had sheep for company in the next field. Snoop got very excited, his canine instinct telling him to round them up. I told him, no, and he gave me the silent treatment again. I pitched next to a bench and had a tin of Baked Beans & Pork Sausages for dinner.

Being near the motorway, mobile phone coverage was good, and I had been asked to give everyone a journey update in person on Zoom.

As anyone who uses video services such as Zoom probably knows, video eats up your phone data like there's no tomorrow, but I had planned for this. My normal phone plan was 2GB a month as I was normally within range of a Wi-Fi signal, but on the road and particularly in remote spots, free Wi-Fi hotspots would be few and far between. So I bumped my data allowance up to 15GB for the time I was away. I figured this might be a bit of overkill, but I might need it for posting on the blog and Internet searches too. Fortunately, my provider Giffgaff allowed you to change your phone data package on a month-by-month basis, so this was handy.

It was dark by the time I joined the others on Zoom. I used my headtorch as a central light for the tent, and it swung around a little as we chatted about the journey so far. It was great to see everyone and to see Mrs B, in particular, was very special. At the same time, it was a bit strange. Not only was I talking to a bunch of people from a tent in a field in the middle of nowhere, but I could see them too.

Later, as I settled down for the night, there was a rumbling from outside, and the tent filled with light as if someone with a torch was scanning the field. The light got brighter and brighter and I wondered what was happening. I'd seen movies where people were abducted by aliens, and I was half expecting the light to move overhead – was I about to be beamed up to the mothership by little green men?

I cautiously unzipped the tent flap and had a look. In the darkness, I could see a camper van driving erratically over the field towards my tent. In a moment of panic, I realised that my tent was green and the field was green, had the driver seen me at all? Should I make a run for it before I was flattened? Snoop took cover in the rucksack.

It was too much excitement for one night. Thankfully, the driver turned and parked a short distance from the tent. He got out followed by a very large German Shepherd that raced around the field as if it hadn't been out for a month.

'Come 'ere Rover' he commanded and Rover headed off in the other direction.

'Ah'reet mate'. He must have seen my panicked face.

'Ah yes, hello, good to have some company other than the sheep' I offered. His name was George.

He proceeded to tell me that he stopped here often.

'She just lets me drive in an' park me van'.

He explained he owned and rented property locally, and I wondered but didn't ask, why he was driving around at 9pm in a camper van, and not living in one of his houses. Perhaps his wife had kicked him out?

I told him of my journey and destination and asked if there were any local shops or cafes I could visit for breakfast. But as usual, there was nothing close.

'Ere 'av these'

He handed a packet of Oats-So-Simple and a sachet of instant vanilla latte.

'Praps that'll keep yer goin'.

He must have seen the desperation in my eyes.

I thanked him and retreated for the night to the sounds of 'Rover!....   Rover!....   Rover....!'

Alan Loach

Day twelve – Porridge and a Latte

It rained overnight and the day started damp and grey but dry. The sachets of porridge and latte were staring at me saying:

'Eat me!'.

I stared back at them, and my stomach was rumbling.

'I need some help here Snoop'

Why didn't I bring a camping stove? Perhaps if I ran the hot tap in the toilet it would be warm enough? However hot water was likely pulled from the farmhouse over the other side of the field, and it was only just warm when it arrived at the toilet block. Maybe it would work with cold water? I couldn't see warmish or cold water working, so I didn't waste the sachets trying. Perhaps I could ask George in his camper, or the nice lady in the farmhouse to boil a kettle for me. But there was no activity from the camper van or farmhouse at this time in the morning.

Snoop was in deep thought trying to figure it out, but I couldn't wait for his solution.

Appleby was 12 miles away, so I Googled cafes in that area and spotted the River Eden Café which had good reviews:

> *Visited for breakfast, recommend the full English with the black pudding and Cumberland sausage the highlights. Great tea and coffee too all served by friendly staff.*

Another said:

> *Great food, great host, Covid aware and very welcoming. This is a cafe you must visit. Dont go to the one next door*

That sounded very promising. I was a big fan of the spirally Cumberland sausage, especially the real stuff from Cumbria. I had worked in the Lakes as a teenager and acquired a taste for it.

The prospect of food made me pack up a little faster, so I shook the water off my tent, packed up and headed off just after 8am.

'Let's get going Snoop, there's a Cumberland sausage waiting for us!'

Although I was feeling a little lethargic this morning, I was ready for my Cumberland Sausage breakfast, and the thought of it spurred me on.

We bid goodbye to the sheep in the next field and headed off. The weather today was overcast but dry and the air was fresh and clean after the rain during the night. The cloud base was low and the south-westerly breeze moved the grey mass swiftly over the landscape. The wind would be behind me for a time, and I was grateful for this.

Today was just short of sixty miles and the elevation half of what it was yesterday, so an easy day in store hopefully. I headed east, the route today would swing back around to the west after Appleby then head north to Penrith.

I was now cycling through the Great Asby Scar National Nature Reserve which was designated an SSSI – a Site of Special Scientific Interest. An important site for its variety of wildlife and plant life including rare species of buckler ferns and limestone ferns. I didn't have time to stop and do some plant spotting however.

The route was dramatic and isolated with views of Wild Boar Fell and the Howgills, a great place for a picnic apparently, and for a walk around the limestone pavement of Great Asby Scar – but not today.

'Alan... come and get me!' I heard in the distance.

It was the Cumberland sausage calling. I peddled a little faster.

At 9.30 I was so pleased to see Appleby on the horizon and I tracked down the Eden River Café.

The ladies in the café were very friendly, and I told them a little about my trip.

'We don't get too many LEJOG cyclists over 'ere in Appleby Love. Mostly they go over Shap close to t' M6'.

It was true, anyone I had spoken to about LEJOG had mentioned Shap as being one of the tougher cycle stages. Shap sat at the highest point on the M6, just north of Tebay where I turned east. Most road LEJOGers would continue to follow the A6 which runs parallel to the M6. My route was going around instead of over and was a little more picturesque.

I ordered a full Cumbrian Breakfast and a Latte. The breakfast included, as I expected, a huge spiral Cumberland Sausage. Snoop was amazed at the size of the sausage. With him being a chef, you would have thought he'd have seen one before.

'There yer go Love, get that down yer. Looks like yer need it.'

I did get it down me. But it concerned me that it looked like I needed it. Was I looking drawn and underfed? In any case, it was delicious!

Then after stocking up on food and goodies from the local Spar, I headed off towards Penrith.

NCN71 headed west out of Appleby, and the Sustrans book warned readers that the next ten miles were quite hard going with several valleys to cross. However, I didn't find the route too difficult. Perhaps my legs were toughening up? I was heading back towards the M6 now and cycling parallel to it towards Penrith.

The cycling today was proving much easier than yesterday. Last night's campsite was at 900 ft and shortly after leaving the road rose to 1200 ft. After this the trajectory was mostly downhill, ending up near sea level at Carlisle.

As I approached Penrith, Brougham Castle was en route and looked imposing in its location next to the River Eamont. The castle inspired a painting by Turner and was featured in a couple of the works of William Wordsworth. The sun broke through as I cycled past, so I stopped for a couple of photographs.

Cycling into Penrith brought memories flooding back. I had cycled through here once before with my good friend Keith in 2010.

It was Keith who re-introduced me to cycling at the age of 48: We were working in Aviemore at a kids' summer camp and he'd brought along his bike; a Ridgeback Velocity. Keith was a retired Professor from Strathclyde University, older than me, but a very active guy. In his tone of voice and mannerisms, he always reminded me of the actor Richard Wilson, of 'One Foot in the Grave' fame, but without the grumpiness.

We chatted about cycling and how I used to enjoy it.

'Have a go!' he said

So I jumped on his bike and took off down the camp driveway. I was like a duck to water; memories came flooding back of days when I would just take off and cycle from Wemyss Bay to Largs or up the coast to Gourock. The sense of freedom and the wind in my hair was amazing! In the 1980s the roads were much quieter and I would cycle helmet-less up and down the A78 coast road. I dread to think of how dangerous that would be these days.

Leaving Keith stranded, the camp driveway and road beyond were only about half a mile long, and when I reluctantly turned around and cycled back up to the camp he was laughing at the huge grin on my face.

'I don't have any hair now to feel the wind in it, but I think I need a bike,' I told him.

And that was it, I was well and truly re-bitten by the cycling bug. I was so impressed by the agility and feel of Keith's bike that I purchased my own Ridgeback Velocity through the Cycle-to-Work Scheme.

Keith was always on the go. He had a real sense of adventure and organised his trips down to the very last detail. I remember him telling me that when he planned to walk the Camino de Santiago, by himself, he had everything weighed out to the last gram so that he wasn't carrying any more than necessary.

'How do you fancy cycling the C to C?' Keith asked one day.

'I guess it's a progression from riding A to B!' I responded in a pathetic joke attempt. I hadn't heard of it.

'It's a coast-to-coast cycle route, from Whitehaven on the west coast to Newcastle on the east coast' Keith explained.

'Train from Glasgow to Whitehaven via Carlisle, a hundred and forty-mile cycle through the Lake District, over the Pennines and down into Newcastle. Then the train back to Glasgow via Edinburgh.'

It sounded amazing. He had tapped into my sense of adventure and I immediately agreed to join him.

'Count me in, when do we go?'

We cycled the Sustrans C to C, or Sea to Sea route from west to east in August 2010 over three days, through Penrith as I was doing today, albeit cycling west to east and not south to north. I remembered that the hill to the east of the town towards the Pennines was rather steep. But I wasn't going this way today.

It was an amazing trip, despite getting thoroughly soaked on the west side of the Pennines, and my knee swelling like a balloon just before reaching the finish.

Sadly, Keith was no longer with us, but he would have loved the idea of doing LEJOG. Had he been around, he may have done it with me.

I stood now in the centre of Penrith remembering his wit, wisdom and sense of humour and the good time we had on our three-day adventure. I stopped in the town centre for a coffee, and I could visualise him cycling towards me as I stood there, a big toothy grin on his face.

At the end of our C to C trip, he told me he had a heart condition and shouldn't have been cycling at all – hearing this I nearly had a heart attack myself!

I was looking forward to the next part of this route, now on NCN7, it was mostly downhill to Carlisle and my stop for the night. The route was what I expected, quiet country roads, rolling countryside, and stone bridges over meandering rivers.

On one part of the route, I spotted some very well-groomed sheep and had to do a double-take.

'Snoop are those real sheep?'

They stood completely still, had completely black heads and legs, and perfectly groomed close-knit coats. They had to be statues or some kind of artwork. I stopped to take a photo and they all turned around to look at me. It was a bit like the original Midwich Cuckoos movie, only with sheep in place of blond alien children. I could tell Snoop was sniggering.

I got to Dalston, four miles from Carlisle. At this point, NCN7 diverted onto a cycle track that followed the River Caldew to the city centre. I paused for a minute. Should I stay on the road or take the cycle path? My experience of cycle paths lined with murderous nettles, and less-than-smooth surfaces hadn't been good to this point, and the road was relatively quiet.... I chose the road, and it was mainly downhill, so I zipped down into Carlisle in no time at all.

My destination was four miles west of Carlisle city centre in the middle of the countryside, but only two miles off my route.

I thought I would be sensible this time and try and get something to eat before I got there. A Google search revealed an Indian and a Chinese restaurant, and a fish & chip shop on the way, so I headed off in anticipation trying not to drool. The Friary Fish & Chips was first. Yes, fish & chips! That would be amazing.

'Sorry Closed on Monday', was the sign on the door.

Next was the Lucky Chop Suey House. Perhaps this was my lucky day? Maybe a nice Chow Mein, or perhaps a Char Sui Pork dish, with a side of spring rolls?

'Sorry Closed on Monday'. No luck. I was in despair, the Indian Take-Away was my only hope.

'Closed,' it said. Just closed – no explanation, just closed!

'Don't people in Carlisle eat on a Monday Snoop?'. It was a rhetorical question, but he seemed to raise his eyebrows in response.

I continued to the campsite: The Wall Lodges & Campsite. I had scoured the area before leaving home looking for a site just north of Carlisle but drew a blank, then I found this site. The site was four miles along NCN72 which headed west out of Carlisle and followed the Cumbrian coast around to Ravenglass. Fortunately, from here I would only have to cycle two miles back to pick up my route again. Unlike in Devon where I plummeted down then back up a valley to the North town Farm campsite when diverting two miles from my route, this diversion was almost flat.

It was a good choice; the site was lovely. Enthusiastic owner Pete showed me the very clean facilities, and there was a shared cabin area with a kettle and food! You could buy snacks and instant breakfasts and drinks, but I had my own from the previous night. So I could have my Oats-So-Simple and the latte sachet the next morning for breakfast, amazing!

Pete must have been desperate to talk to someone as I got a rundown of many of the campers who were staying the night and their destinations, and even a history of the campsite and how it was built over a Roman fort after excavations on the site. Hence the name of the site.

'We are only allowed to use the area where you are for tents. The ruins under the ground might be disturbed by cars and campers'

So I was camping on top of an actual Roman Camp. Interesting!

I was about to pose my usual question about local places to eat or if any delivery service reached out this far, but he beat me to it, and without taking a breath launched into a promo of the local pub, The Drovers Rest.

'They do amazing food; will I book a table for you?'.

I paused with the memory of the minuscule portions at the Coach & Horses.

'Is it a restaurant or do they do bar meals?' I asked. Deriving the logic that bar meals are likely to be less refined but proportionally larger in the quantity of food to a posh restaurant.

He confirmed it was bar meals and in an instant was on the phone to the place booking a table for me.

'Tell them Pete from the campsite sent you'.

Perhaps he was on some kind of commission? It didn't matter, I was starving!

The pub was a five-minute walk. The Drover's Rest was a 400-year-old country pub with what seemed like original wooden beams along the ceiling, a large open fire and an equally large dog sprawled out asleep in the middle of the floor. I stepped over the dog and it woke up momentarily with a vague interest in who I was and then went back to sleep again.

I ordered a homemade burger, which was the size of a curling stone. It came with a mountain of chips, battered onion rings, and some homemade coleslaw. I was in heaven!

I had done well for food today and waddled back to the campsite.

Then after chatting with a couple of people who were walking Hadrian's Wall, calling Mrs B, and crawling back into my tent with a full stomach, I fell asleep.

Miles of Memories

Day thirteen – Across the Border

I was well into my morning camping routine now. I would wake, have a look outside, sprint to the toilet to empty my Oasis bottle and roll up my sleeping bag and mat. Deflate my pillow and look at what I had in my bags for breakfast.

'Wait a minute', you might ask, 'what Oasis bottle?' ...

I found out early on in my trip that there had to be a better way than trekking all the way to the toilet block in the middle of the night. It wasn't so bad if the toilets were close by but going in the middle of the night involved getting my shoes on, strapping the head torch to my head if the site wasn't well-lit, and trekking there and back. I found I was wide awake after this. Because they say you need to be careful not to get dehydrated when cycling I was drinking gallons during the day and as a consequence, nature could call up to three times in one night. So, something had to be done.

I wondered... You get porta-potties for camping, but did they do something even more portable for hikers and cyclists? I did a Google search and to my amusement found items labelled 'Camping Travel Pee Bags'. Reassuringly it stated that 'liquid is absorbed by the gel within sixty seconds'. It showed pictures of situations where it could be used: tents, traffic jams and a child in the back seat of a car being sick. So glad they didn't reveal more pictures of its usage! Another was the 'Shrinkable Emergency Urinal', a concertina-type device that stretched as it filled 'extends to 12.2 inches' it boasted.

'So what do you do for a living?'

'I design camping travel pee bags….' I think this could be a bit of a conversation-stopper.

Anyway, all these things are just containers, and even if I did want one, Amazon wasn't going to deliver to my tent, so I decided to find something of suitable dimensions which would save me the trek to the loo in the middle of the night.

On a visit to a supermarket, I spotted a bottle of Oasis, which looked dimensionally agreeable, so I took it to the cashier to pay. I usually chat with cashiers. With Mrs B having experience of being such a cashier, they are often taken for granted or completely ignored as people rush through with their shopping, often on the phone, not saying so much as a thank-you to the person serving them.

After asking how their day was going (the usual question, but better than no question at all) my attention turned to the bottle and its use after I had drunk the contents.

Snoop gave me a glance that said, 'No Alan, you can't mention what you're going to use the bottle for...' I stopped myself in my tracks.

So this morning at some point I had to perform my ninja stealth trip to the toilets with my Oasis bottle. I couldn't be seen in possession of a bottle of yellow Oasis, because there's no such thing. It felt like I was smuggling drugs across the campsite, so I would carefully scan the surroundings before exiting the tent and sprint to the toilet block hoping I wouldn't be stopped or meet someone on the way.

'Excuse me, is that lemon & lime flavoured Oasis?'

I was never asked this but thought I should have an answer ready, just in case.

'Ah, no it's not Oasis, but Fairy Liquid. You know the lemon stuff'

'Erm... it's an experimental flavour... '

'Yes Lemon & Lime, would you like to try it?'

Today I exited the tent to find the guy from the next tent lying in his sleeping bag in the middle of the grass, my ninja run stalled until later.

I met him and his wife the evening before, this was their starting point for walking the Hadrian's Wall Trail. The previous evening they were having a 'discussion' about the things they had forgotten to bring, and this morning he was out of his tent.

'Are you OK?' I asked, wondering if he'd fallen out with his other half, and she'd chucked him out. He was staring at the sky.

'Absolutely amazing!' he answered, 'been watching the stars for hours'.

It was sunrise and the stars were disappearing now, but he was right, in the middle of the countryside, away from the street lighting of the town and cities, the stars were like a carpet of lights gracing the Heavens.

I made my way to the shared area cabin and boiled the kettle for my Oat So Simple and Latte sachet. Warm food. Such a luxury which I took for granted every day at home.

Many of the other campers, most of whom were also walking the Wall, were up and about too, and I figured this could be another walking adventure with Mrs B or a cycle trip someday.

Setting off I had done another reroute from the Sustrans route in the book over the Solway estuary and had managed to cut ten miles off my route up to the Scottish border.

I cycled the two miles back along NCN72 towards Carlisle, then across the River Eden, to rejoin NCN7.

Back on track and once again heading north, the view southwest over the Solway estuary took in the northern Lake District peaks. I stopped to look at the light glistening on the water, imagining the incredible sunsets that must occur over the Firth from this vantage point.

The route continued along NCN7 crossing the River Esk, over which Thomas Telford built his famous Metal Bridge. The original bridge was built in 1815-1823 as part of the West Coast Great North Road. However, the structure was now long gone, only a small settlement named Metal Bridge remained along with an inn of the same name. A replacement bridge carrying the M6 motorway now crossed the river nearby, and I crossed the river on an attached minor-road bridge. The Scottish Border was not far away.

The minor road ran parallel to the motorway for a couple of miles and the signs for Gretna appeared, followed by the border signpost.

'Snoop, this is a proud moment. We've cycled the length of England!' I couldn't quite believe it. Although the furthest point north in England was on the east coast at Berwick-Upon-Tweed, I had still reached the border. The border post displayed the miles to both Land's End and John O'Groats,

'Land's End 478 miles' it said rather confusingly – I had cycled at this point about 700 miles! There was no indication of how this mileage was arrived at, but I guess it must have been the shortest possible distance by road. Or perhaps this figure was 'as the crow flies'?

Mr Google would know, of course, so I quickly plotted a route in Google Maps from Gretna to Land's End. Mr Google's route for a car managed to shave a mile off the signpost mileage and gave me 477 miles. M6, M5, A30, done. If it was allowed, the thought of cycling down the motorways appealed in many ways. The gradients would be gentler, the roads straighter, and the hold-ups probably zero.

I imagined flying along the hard shoulder past a twenty-mile vehicle tailback. That would be amazing! On the negative side, miles and miles of motorway might get a little boring.

Interestingly, or perhaps not, Mr Google's cycle route was 533 miles and the walking route was 462 miles.

'Snoop, we're back in Scotland!' He didn't seem very moved, but I detected a feeling of silent joy.

I rolled over the border into Dumfries and Galloway, into the town of Gretna and stocked up on the usual supplies from a local shop.

Gretna was built to house 30,000 employees of what was the biggest munitions factory in the world during the First World War. It stretched nine miles along the Solway Coast and produced an explosive mix called cordite, which was nicknamed Devil's Porridge. A museum of the same name told the story. Of course, I didn't have time to investigate.

Perhaps more famously, the nearby Gretna Green, since 1754, was where young English runaway couples eloped to, so they could be married 'over the anvil' from the age of 16. The Famous Blacksmiths Shop, where the ceremonies were conducted, was still there. At the time of writing, around 5,000 couples tied the knot in the area every year. That would be about 100 marriages every week, which definitely earns it the title of 'marriage capital of the UK'.

Today's route ran pretty much parallel to the M74 on NCN74 starting from sea level on the Solway Firth estuary, then rising gradually to the Beatock Summit at 1200ft. It was uphill most of the way today, but Komoot suggested that the gradients were mostly in the green zone with a couple of oranges and only one red.

Now I was over the border I knew one thing - it was pretty much a straight road all the way to Glasgow. No problems taking wrong turns or going around in circles as the roads were going to get very familiar, and I'd be able to zip along a bit faster than before. The weather was sunny and calm and I pretty much had the single-track roads to myself.

My first stop was the village of Ecclefechan, known locally as simply 'Fechan', whose name always mystified me in the past when travelling along the M74. It's said that the name was derived from the Brythonic or Celtic for 'small church'. But legend also had it that it took its name from the village being dedicated to the seventh century Irish saint, St Féchín of Fore.

Like many towns and villages along this stretch of road, it was once a staging post for travellers making their way from England to Scotland, or vice-versa, but had now been bypassed.

Lockerbie loomed after a while, it was probably the most obvious place to stop for lunch, even though it was a little too early for lunch. Lockerbie was, of course, the place of the tragic air crash several years ago, but I had never been into the town. These days it's easy to bypass as you drive down the M74. For many drivers, when on a motorway, the preference is one of the purpose-built quick stop-off services, with fuel, coffee, and burgers on tap from early morning to late at night.

The attraction of Lockerbie on my journey was found through Google Maps. Looking for a coffee shop, I found out that the town had a Greggs. Ideal, they do coffee, sandwiches, and pastries. That sounded like a good lunch to me, so I got one of each: a caramel latte, a chicken mayo baguette, and a steak bake. I sat on a bench in the town square in the sunshine to eat them, surrounded by life-size metal sculptures of sheep.

'Fancy a ride on a sheep Snoop?' I think he would have gone for it, but he was in one of his silent moods.

I guess investment must have been poured into the town over the years following the tragedy. Perhaps I was expecting a town still in mourning, so it surprised me that the atmosphere in the town was so peaceful and calm.

North of Lockerbie, NCN74 followed the B7076, which was the old A74 and the landscape was best described as rolling, a gradual gradient that took me higher and higher up into wind-turbine country. I've known people who hate these gentle giants with a passion, but I rather like them as they gracefully turn, capturing the power of the wind and converting it cleanly into the electricity we all use.

I passed the town of Moffat, where I had considered camping at one point. If I had been cycling via Edinburgh or the Borders, I would have turned off my cycle route here and headed north-east through dramatic mountainous scenery, and past the Grey Mares Tail, the fifth-highest waterfall in the UK. However, I would be staying parallel to the M74 today and heading north-west towards Glasgow.

I climbed steadily to 1200ft, the Beatock summit and the air was cooler and fresher at this altitude. The transport routes of motorway, cycle route and railway crossed over and under each other, competing for the route through the valley between the hills. I had travelled this route on the adjacent motorway many times by car, but not by bike before. When travelling north through this part of the country, the roll of the hills and the texture of the countryside with its vast plantations of evergreens always reminded me of the remote but wonderful spaces that can be found in Scotland.

The road plateaued after Beatock, then started a gradual decline into South Lanarkshire passing through the small remote village of Elvanfoot. The source of the River Clyde ran close by.

Elvanfoot was developed as a road and rail junction in the early twentieth century, with a line branching west to the lead mines of Leadhills and Wanlockhead.

'Lovely up here, Snoop, but must be chilly in winter'. He agreed. The sense of remoteness was only tarnished by the M74 cutting its way through the peaceful landscape. But I guessed some people would like the combination of remoteness and easy access to the motorway network.

I think my legs were getting used to this cycling thing, and I soon reached Abington and my stop for the night at the Hill View Caravan & Camping site. The elevation was still almost 1000ft, but it didn't seem like it. I was surprised at how busy the site was, but it was a beautiful site, nestled in the hills. Another £10 a night. Good value, clean, and safe.

I had called Mrs B earlier in the day when I realised that the campsite was only a 45-minute drive from home.

'How would you like to come down and take me out for dinner?' I said. She was thrilled at the idea.

'You'll need to give me the postcode' she replied.

Google Maps didn't like the campsite's postcode so I gave her a postcode for a car park in Abington to put in her satnav. We would meet at 7pm.

The lady in the site office recommended a local place to eat, and sang it's praises highly, but then remembered that they were closed on Tuesdays.

'Not many options around here I'm afraid. Only the motorway services at this time of night'.

It was still early evening, but I guess that's how it is in rural areas.

Mrs B arrived and we visited the motorway services for our reunion dinner. Harry Ramsden's Fish & Chips were quite good for a motorway service area. However, I guess anything would have tasted good after almost two weeks of eating tins of cold beans, and tuna pots.

When we got back to the campsite, she surveyed the state I was in with my shredded legs and developing tan lines. The middle of my hands were completely white from the fingerless gloves and my fingers and arms were a deepening brown colour. My legs were going the same way. I'm just glad the sun hadn't created patches of brown through the holes in my cycle helmet.

Mrs B pointed out a cosy-looking wooden chalet.

'Snoop says he wants to stay there for the night or come home with me'

We chatted for a while, took some photos, and then she was off home to her comfy bed leaving Snoop behind. We would see each other again tomorrow.

Miles of Memories

Day fourteen – Take a break

The rising sun lit up the tent for the start of day 14. I zipped open the tent to be greeted by an early sunrise with the first rays catching the tops of the hills and casting long shadows on the grass. I stretched and breathed in the fresh morning air.

It was hard to believe the campsite was only about a mile from the M74, there was such an air of peace and tranquillity. I took several photos and packed up looking forward to the day ahead. Only fifty miles today and I would be stopping for lunch with friends and meeting up with Mrs B again.

I headed through Abington and under the M74 onto the A74 or NCN74. So eager to get going, that I forgot to stop at the Abington services for my morning coffee.

Sections of the road now used as a cycle route were once the old A74 duel carriageway which not so long ago, before the motorway upgrade, carried lots of traffic between Scotland and England. Sometimes the old road would run parallel to the motorway, but at other times the motorway took a completely different route, and the old road was left stranded in what seemed like the middle of nowhere.

This was ideal wind farm country, exposed and unobstructed by large hills. I passed the relatively small Middle Muir wind farm, the graceful giant blades of the turbines seemed to turn slowly as I cycled along. Their size however was deceptive. It's only up close that you can see the sheer size of the structures and blade tips that can cut through the air at speeds of over 100mph.

As I headed towards Lesmahagow, I found my coffee as the old road converged again with the motorway at Cairn Lodge Services. The Shell petrol station shop did coffee-to-go, and I had a large vanilla latte.

I remember driving the old A74 regularly in the late 1970s. I lived in Ayrshire with my parents, and when I left school and passed my driving test, I went to catering college in Blackpool and then worked briefly in a hotel in the Lake District on placement from college.

On my days off, I would zoom up and down this road in my dark blue 850cc Mini (reg: YHH 11K), often getting up in the middle of the night to arrive at 7am for breakfast to surprise everyone at home.

This was my second car, the first was also an Austin Mini 850 (reg: 303 TE) first manufactured in 1962 with features such as horizontally sliding windows in the driver and passenger doors, a push button next to the handbrake to start the car and a foot-operated headlight dipping switch next to the clutch pedal (found by accident one day!). A real classic which came to an untimely demise after being lent to a work colleague.

I don't know if anyone else can remember the registration numbers of their first cars, but they somehow have been imprinted in my memory.

On arriving at 7am to surprise my family...

'Hello Ali, good to see you'.

My family always called me Ali, which didn't really work in Scotland. North of the border Ali would be short for Alistair, not Alan.

'Want some breakfast?'

They never showed any surprise at my 7am arrival. Mum and Dad were pretty chilled people, and never really batted an eyelid at what I did. Not that they didn't care. Having brought up three kids before I arrived, they'd seen it all before.

As I cycled this road, memories came flooding back. There was one point on the road where it dipped and passed through Lesmahagow. Here I would put my foot down and use all of those 850ccs to build up momentum to get the car up the hill at the other end of the town without changing down a gear.

I sat at the top of this same hill now, on my bike, looking at the dip in the road and the hill on the other side. I'm sure the hill was bigger in the 1970s, but I knew what I had to do.

'Foot to the floor Snoop, we're about to hit that hill in top gear'

We set off at breakneck speed down into the dip and towards the hill in top gear (which would be number 27 on my bike). I peddled furiously and Snoop was clinging on for his life. Pedestrians scattered as I flew along and babies in pushchairs burst into tears (not really – I just made that last bit up). We reached the hill and flew up it, reaching the crest without changing down.

'We did it Snoop'. I say 'we'; it was me who was doing all the hard work.

In reality, it wasn't such a big hill after all, but knowing I'd beaten it in top gear was nonetheless satisfying. Great memories!

After Lesmahagow, I diverted a couple of miles to meet with friends Alan & Fran who put on an amazing lunch for Mrs B and me, with soup, sandwiches, scones, and strawberries. I'm not sure the food alliteration was planned, but nevertheless, it was an amazing treat.

We had become good friends with Alan & Fran during my years at art college and we would all go on arty days out to places like Pittenweem, for the yearly art festival.

Fran was the arty one. She produced delightful abstract works full of colour and texture. We had several exhibitions together, and it would be Fran who sold most paintings. In recent years, however, for me, working for a living had hampered my creativity, but I always had the desire to get back to being creative again.

Four years at art college had been good and bad for my creativity. I was told once that art college can kill your natural talent. Although that maybe didn't happen to me, I think the best way to describe it was that it muddied my talent, throwing in too many options and choices into my creativity, and leaving me not knowing what direction to take.

Lunch was finished and I felt a few stones heavier, but it was totally worth it.

'Do you want a lift?' Mrs B said.

She was testing me, and I looked at Snoop who had a 'don't you dare' look on his face.

'Absolutely not, I need to cycle it'

'Thought so. Just thought I would ask'

'But you can take my rucksack!'.

I waved goodbye to everyone and headed downhill towards Hamilton. It was good to travel a little lighter for the next 30 miles,

The Sustrans route in the book followed the NCN7 westward, along the Clyde Valley through Glasgow, to Clydebank and Bowling, before swinging north and north-east past Loch Lomond, the Trossachs, then Callander, through Killin and along Loch Tay. A lovely, picturesque journey, and probably some of the best scenery of the whole route. However, I didn't intend to go this way, having done this route before. I planned to divert north at Hamilton, cross into North Lanarkshire, and head for a day off in Cumbernauld. I would rejoin the Sustrans route a couple of days later at Pitlochry.

As I passed into North Lanarkshire, through Bellshill and my old workplace, I was in very familiar territory. This was my cycle commute from a few years ago. I had 12 miles to go.

I paused near my old place of employment and memories flooded back of my first commute, which came about out of necessity in some ways. This was just after purchasing my Cycle-To-Work scheme bike on Keith's recommendation as mentioned earlier.

Mrs B was going through a period of chronic fatigue when she had to give up work, so our income dropped quite a bit. I figured that if I cycled to work instead of driving, we might save some money, so I started my cycle commute.

I worked out that I could cycle two miles to the train station, take the bike onboard with me for a fifteen-minute train journey, and then cycle a final three miles to work. The return journey would give me a total of ten miles of cycling a day. This sounded possible.

My first commute was entertaining, arriving at work with a grand total of five miles under my belt, my legs had turned to jelly. Who thought this was a good idea? I soon got used to it though and cycled all through the winter of 2008/09, which was thankfully mild.

The commute turned out to be ideal for building up my cycling strength and worked well in most types of weather, except when the trains were cancelled. Then I would be on the phone to Mrs B:

'Come and rescue me please!'

'Give me a postcode' she would say. This was a woman who had no sense of direction whatsoever. The best advice I ever gave her was:

'If you think you should be going in one direction, turn around and go the opposite way'.

She admits that this worked every time.

By the time the spring and summer of 2009 came, I was extending my cycles to ride the whole way to work. 12 miles each way.

Before buying my bike, my car commute consisted of a 15-mile trek down a motorway in the busy rush hour traffic. Cars nose to tail and shuffling along at road junctions and roundabouts. This turned into a nightmare should there be any roadworks, and I would get to work drained and agitated from the drive, dreading the journey home at the end of the day.

This all changed when I started cycle commuting, and I found the art was in choosing the right route. In planning a cycling route there's no point in thinking like a motorist. This didn't work. I wanted to stay as far away from busy roads as possible.

The app I used at the time was Cyclestreets, which is still out there, but perhaps getting a bit dated now. You would choose your starting point and destination, and perhaps a waypoint. Then the app would calculate your route, prioritising cycle paths and quiet roads to get you to your destination.

For my commute, the app chose some very quiet farm roads for a large stretch of the journey, and I would zip along this route knowing that a short distance away could be irate car commuters with their blood pressure rising. It was a refreshing change, as nothing, apart from an occasional puncture, not roadworks, traffic jams, or accidents could hold you back. I could time my journey and always arrive on time.

Fast forward a few years, a redundancy, four years doing art at college, and a new job, and I had been cycle-commuting for quite a while, so had a generally good level of cycling fitness. My commute was now 14 miles which I did some days, combined with partial cycle commutes. The partial commutes consisted of putting the bike in the back of the car, driving part of the way, parking up somewhere, and cycling the rest of the way. The choice was a bit weather, and time of the year dependent.

Today I continued my cycle with 12 miles to go, which on the scale of my current cycle seemed like nothing at all.

Arriving home, it was great to spend the evening and a whole day with Mrs B, but it felt a bit like cheating. I should be out there in my tent.

Mrs B made sure I had everything I needed to continue, she bought me some cream for my chaffed backside, and she patiently unpicked the padding out of my cycling shorts. She knew me better than I knew myself and often got things ready for me before I even realised I needed them. I don't know what I would have done without her.

The amazing thing about my day at home was that it poured with rain, a truly miserable day. It hadn't rained at all in the first fourteen days while I was cycling. It had rained overnight a couple of times, and I had a couple of brief bouts of damp mist, but while on the bike – no rain.

Pondering the challenge of the next few days brought back memories of my cycle from home to Inverness in 2013. We planned it as a mini-holiday over 5 days. I did the cycling, and Mrs B was my backup driver. It worked well at the time. We stayed in B&Bs. I headed off on my bike early in the morning and cycled for four or five hours. Meanwhile, Mrs B, not being a morning person, got up a little later and browsed the local shops before catching up with me in the car at lunchtime. We then spent the afternoon and evening together and repeated this each day.

For this 2013 trip, I followed the Forth & Clyde Canal to the Falkirk Wheel, then headed north through Stenhousemuir, and picked up NCN76 to Stirling. Then cycled on roads parallel to the busy A84 to Callander to pick up NCN7 on its way to Pitlochry.

This was a great route, but having done it before and being on a tight schedule this time I chose a more direct route: Cumbernauld, Denny, Stirling, Dunblane, Perth then Pitlochry and Aviemore over 2 days. It took me 4 days to go this far in 2013! I pondered this. Could I do it in 2 days?

Beyond Pitlochry, I would be cycling the same route as in 2013 to Inverness on NCN7. Another magnificent cycle in itself.

Snoop was enjoying the rest too, and we posted photos on the blog of his new eBay bike, a nice bright blue number to match his waterproofs. Quite the fashion guru.

Two nights at home was a real luxury, but I was itching to get back on the road and keep the momentum going. At night, my leg muscles were twitching and those giant

Jelly Babies in my dreams were now running off ahead of me. I shouted at them:

'Slow down! Wait for me!'

Alan Loach

Day fifteen – Bear Necessities

After a relaxing day at home, I was raring to get going on my final leg; six more days to John O'Groats. Today's destination was Perth, again on familiar roads.

My training for LEJOG was in a sixty-mile radius from home, and I'd probably travelled most of the roads around here, if not on the bike, certainly in the car. My nature was always to explore.

'I wonder where this road goes?' I would think to myself and I would be off down single-track roads, farm roads, paths, and old railway lines. Part of this came from driving to and from work.

A pet hate of mine was traffic, particularly queues or jams. I would try and find an alternative route to avoid such situations, and in the process had come to know all the shortcuts and back roads in the local area.

When I rediscovered cycling it was such a pleasure travelling these back roads. Zipping along free of traffic.

Mrs B saw me off again.

'See you in a week. Cycle carefully!'

Up to lunchtime today, I would know all the roads – I'd cycled these many times not only in training but simply exploring. Today I had a special lunch planned in Dunblane.

I set off passing under the Castlecary Arches, a Victorian railway viaduct which opened in 1842. The Arches spanned and towered above the M80 and other minor roads and were one of the most distinctive features of the Edinburgh and Glasgow Railway. In doing so I also crossed the line of the Antonine Wall.

The Roman-built Antonine Wall from the second century stretched between the Firth of Forth and the Firth of Clyde. The wall was a northerly version of Hadrian's Wall, constructed as a turf fortification with wooden forts on stone foundations. Because the wall itself wasn't of stone or brick construction, over the centuries much of it had been demolished and flattened with agricultural activity, the building of settlements, and to make way for the canals and railways.

This was very familiar territory, as for part of my recent art degree I had been studying the route that Saint Mungo took from Culross to Glasgow in the sixth century. His route would have crossed and probably followed part of the Antonine Wall. Mungo's life was surrounded by much folklore; born in Culross and becoming the patron saint of Glasgow, he must have walked between the two locations. I was intrigued to try and discover his route. So I researched and plotted a route of where he might have walked and then I walked it. The result inspired me to start another book, following the footsteps of Saint Mungo, which has yet to be completed.

The weather today had brightened from the previous day's rain and there was a freshness in the air. It was early September and the countryside was at its peak as it headed towards Autumn.

The hedgerows and the canal were teeming with wildlife. Heron were a familiar sight on the canal and would take off on the approach of the bike, gracefully gliding to the opposite bank. Close to the more wooded areas, kingfishers could be seen darting along the canal, a neon blue flash and gone. Passing the canal locks, narrowboats plied up and down, their passengers choosing a slower pace of life. It all looked very appealing.

The Forth & Clyde Canal path stretched the whole way across Central Scotland (NCN754) and I had cycled every inch of it. I remember once cycling it with my son Tim, heading east to cycle over the Forth Road Bridge near Edinburgh. The bridge is now closed to cars, which now use the new Queensferry crossing, but back then the bridge was very busy with every kind of road traffic thundering over it. The experience of cycling over it was a little scary as the bridge constantly shook and bounced with the motion of the traffic. We were heading for St Andrews on the east coast, stopping overnight in a Travelodge in Glenrothes, and getting the train back from Forres.

It was another great cycle apart from Tim having an encounter with a wall and ending up with gashes on his arm. But we both survived to cycle another day.

Turning reluctantly off the canal at Bonnybridge and heading north, I passed through Denny, into Stirlingshire, and through Bannockburn to arrive in Stirling, a city with more than its fair share of Scottish history.

Its medieval Stirling Castle sat high on a craggy volcanic rock next to the city centre. A couple of miles away on another rocky outcrop called Abbey Craig, the National Wallace Monument, was another familiar structure on the Stirlingshire skyline. Visitors could climb its amazing spiral staircase to be treated to panoramic views of Stirling and the Forth Valley. Below could be seen the site of the 1297 Battle of Stirling Bridge, where William

Wallace defeated the English, and Bannockburn, the site of another famous battle in 1314.

I continued north to Bridge of Allan and headed up and over the hill on the Old Glen Road to Dunblane.

Lunch stop today was at Zee's in Dunblane, my favourite daughter - actually my only daughter. She made a wonderful pasta bake with chicken and pasta and cheese and other good stuff. Snoop was very impressed and wanted the recipe. It was truly delicious and set me up for the remaining cycle to Perth. She sent me off with encouraging words.

'Go Dad. You can do it!'

Yes, I could do it, the cycling was getting easier now, and my legs felt like they were getting stronger. I was aware that there may still be setbacks with two eighty-plus mile days coming up, but I was on a mission and I felt that nothing could hold me back.

Reading some of the advice on doing LEJOG, many people said that they got much fitter the further they travelled. I guess it made sense that you're pushing yourself day after day, and your body has a choice: adapt to the daily pounding and get stronger, or cave in to the daily pounding and give up. I was so glad that my body seemed to be building itself up. Those same people said that Cornwall and Devon were definitely the hardest part of the journey. The hills were blamed for this, and I can see the logic in this: some of the hills in the southwest were killers. But I wonder if they wouldn't have seemed so formidable if I were to go back to them after finishing LEJOG with my toughened-up legs? I noted to myself that I must find someone who had done it the other way around, John O'Groats to Land's End, and ask them about their experience of the hills at the end of their cycle in Cornwall.

I headed out of Dunblane, once a Victorian Spa town, passing under the busy A9 onto the much quieter back roads. I was heading into the Perthshire countryside, another county line crossed, and the roads led me through to the village of Braco, where a church tower stood alone without a church.

The story went that Ardoch Free Church, built in 1782, was struck by lightning and had to be demolished for safety reasons. So the Tower now stands alone operating as a clock tower. I noted the correct time on the clock as I passed, so it looked like it was still maintained and working.

My route was running parallel to the busy A9, but not so close that the traffic was visible or even within earshot. The rolling Perthshire hills were delightful, and I was making very good time.

On my previous evening at home, I reviewed my final routes on the computer and figured that some of the routes I had planned from the book could be rerouted. I poured over Google Maps and Streetview to try and streamline them.

With hindsight, some of this worked, and some didn't, there is no substitute for getting out there and scouting them out for yourself. I had done this for the previous 2013 cycle trip. Mrs B and I drove from Cumbernauld to Inverness as much as possible along the route I would cycle looking for the best route, but the same couldn't be easily applied to the length of the whole country.

Not far away was Auchterarder, home of the 5-star Gleneagles Hotel and golf course. I would have graced them with my presence but figured that Hi-Viz and black might not be an appropriate dress code for such a high-class establishment. Mrs B and I once stopped off here out of curiosity, but £40 each for afternoon tea was a little beyond our budget.

Two miles north of Auchterarder, I rode over the Kinkell Bridge built in 1793, a handsome four-arched bridge over the River Earn. I paused for a snack and took in the tranquillity of the water flowing gently under the bridge, the ducks tended to their ducklings in the shallows, and sheep on the grassy banks munched on the greenery.

Heading off again for Perth I passed fields full of grouse that scattered as I cycled by, and I passed through several wooded areas.

Cycling through a particularly dense patch of woodland, suddenly my eye caught sight of something in the woods. I screeched to a halt.

'Snoop, was that a bear?'

Snoop froze in terror, which turns out to be the best thing to do if you meet a wild bear. I did a double-take, and for an instant, a question flashed across my mind:

'Can I cycle faster than a bear can run?'

A good question and one I looked up later. Apparently, a black bear can sprint at more than 30 mph, so I wouldn't have stood much of a chance if there was a bear and it had given chase.

What I actually saw turned out to be the base of a large, uprooted tree which had likely been blown over in a storm.

Bears were native to Scotland at one time, but I was so glad that there were no wild bears in Scotland these days. There again I suppose one could have escaped from captivity...

I was nearing Perth now, and riding along quite happily, pleased with my rerouting until I suddenly ended up on the busy A9. Oops, a bit of a rerouting blunder here!

'Snoop, I think we need to find a different way'

He rolled his eyes in disbelief. There was no way I was cycling along the A9, the main dual carriageway to the north of Scotland, and possibly one of Scotland's busiest roads. There were quieter motorways. Cars, HGVs, buses, and everyone in such a rush, were flying along at the speed limit or more. A cyclist would need to have a death wish to join this traffic.

OK, Mr Google give me a hand here. Google maps showed there was no point in retracing my steps, it was a long way back. However, if I went half a mile along the A9 I could divert onto another side road. I ended up walking along the grass verge to the side road.

I arrived at The Ark campsite on the western edge of Perth sooner than I expected. It was clean and tidy and not too busy with tents. There were more camper vans than anything else, a popular way of holidaying it would seem since Covid arrived.

I originally wasn't going to bother booking any campsites. The logic was that I'd set out for the day, cycle about 60 miles, stop when I got tired and find a local campsite. After all, most sites would probably be able to find a small square of grass for a lone camper, would they not? I would just Google 'campsites' on Google Maps when I stopped and make my way to the nearest. I did a trial search for potential sites along the route where I might stop. However, in the more remote areas, it looked like I might have some issues, and end up cycling either way off route or much further than I wanted to.

In the end, I decided to book sites before I left home. For one, it meant I had a specific destination, plus it was one less unknown to think about, and I could concentrate on cycling.

In reality, with all the sites I had stayed at, I could have just turned up at the gate and secured a pitch, but I didn't know this at the time.

At the Ark campsite, another cyclist arrived as I was pitching the tent. He was a tall wiry guy with a very long beard, older than me. (I'm 29 in my head). Although with myself at sixty years old he couldn't have been much older. For all I knew, maybe he'd just had a hard life and was twenty years younger. Anyway, he was very obviously a seasoned touring cyclist, very tanned and toned.

'Where are you heading?', it was my turn to ask the usual question.

'Oh I've just finished and heading south on the train tomorrow' He replied. 'I've been cycling the west coast of Scotland'

He mentioned going over the Bealach na Bà (the pass of the cattle) near Applecross. I had been over here in the car, and it was quite spectacular. The steepest ascent of any road in the UK. From sea level at Applecross to 2,054 ft in just a couple of miles. Add to this very tight hairpin bends winding up the hillside and gradients approaching 20%; this would be one of those roads that would be a nightmare to cycle up, but a dream to cycle down.

It reminded me of a cycle in the Cairngorms. Mrs B and I were on holiday in Aviemore one year and I got her to drive me up to the Cairngorm Railway car park at just over 2000 ft.

'You want me to leave you here?...'

'Yes I'll see you in an hour at the Potting Shed'

The Potting Shed was a tearoom in the middle of the Cairngorm forests a few miles away. It was famed for its bird-viewing windows where many birds and squirrels would come to eat at the feeders and be photographed by the tourists.

She was gone and I had an amazing cycle down towards Aviemore, and this was only a 1000 ft descent. I noted Applecross as one for the bucket list.

Mr Long Beard seemed to know every inch of every cycle route in Scotland and gave me a few tips on the remainder of my route north. After my diversions today I badly needed that advice.

I considered my route for the next day before falling asleep. I was back on familiar roads for the whole day, having cycled north from Perth some years earlier.

'Snoop, we have a long way to cycle tomorrow. I'll cycle and you can navigate, as I'm clearly not good at it.' He seemed pleased to have something to do and I sensed lots of activity under his little chef's hat.

'Go Snoop, tomorrow's going to be a good day!'

Day sixteen - Head for the Hills

An early start was necessary for day sixteen. Another day of deadlines, why do I do this to myself? This day was one of the longer cycles at eighty-two miles and an estimated ride time of eleven hours including breaks. The reason for the long stretch was the availability of campsites. Today I banked on the fact that although the highest point was 1500ft over the Drumochter Pass, there would be twenty miles of downhill after this to give me a break from pushing too hard.

First off, I had agreed to meet up with good friends Carmen & Alastair in Pitlochry at 10am. I chose the time so I only had myself to blame. The plan was three hours to Pitlochry, a one-hour break, then seven hours with breaks for the next fifty-two miles, over the Drumochter Pass to the campsite at Alvie. I was hoping to get there before 6pm when the site office closed.

'Snoop, we're off again, eighty-two miles today'. He didn't seem bothered by this revelation; he was geared up for his navigation task.

'I think it's your turn to make breakfast'. I prompted. He didn't respond, obviously focussing on the route ahead.

Heading off at 7am, I needed to maintain 10mph to get to Pitlochry at 10am, so I kept a close eye on my progress. Fortunately, the Perthshire landscape north of Perth to Pitlochry affords fairly easy gradients and good roads which were pretty much traffic-free - there was little to hold me back. However at this average speed, I hadn't allowed for any breaks, but I was getting used to just pushing on regardless.

The Perthshire country roads were a delight to cycle along, gently undulating and winding through a landscape of hills and forests.

As I approached Dunkeld, my mind turned to the adjoining town of Birnam which was made famous by Shakespeare in his play Macbeth. In a vision Macbeth was told that he...

"shall never vanquished be, until Great Birnam wood to high Dunsinane hill shall come against him."

There wasn't going to be any vanquishing today, thank you very much, so I pedalled on.

I arrived at Dunkeld, one and a half hours and 15 miles from Perth, so on schedule so far. The mist was rising and I crossed its famous bridge, yet another bridge designed by Thomas Telford. This one was built in 1809.

Dunkeld was a lovely place on the banks of the River Tay, lined with ancient forests, and graced by its own cathedral.

We had stopped in here many times on journeys up and down the A9. Palmerston's cafe here did amazing scones and rock buns, but you needed to be there early as they were made fresh every day and they sold out quickly. Having said that, even if I did have time today, I was too early - they hadn't even opened yet!

I paused for a few minutes with the memories and the tranquillity of my surroundings.

The Perthshire countryside was stunning in every season, but I especially remember driving along the A9 near where I was just now in the autumn with the foliage a spectacular blaze of reds, oranges, and yellows. A sight to behold.

Pitlochry was ahead, a place Mrs B and I had also been to many times. On one occasion we were visiting in October, with the trees full of colour, and in the main street, we saw coaches of people disappearing in the evenings, and other coaches arriving back. We were mystified, Pitlochry was a lovely place but surrounded by countryside. Where would busloads of people be going in the dark? The attraction was the Enchanted Forest. This was a light show set in a local forest, Faskally Woods, where the trees, foliage and loch were used as a backdrop to multicoloured lighting and effects. We booked to go and it was spectacular. It still runs each autumn, but in recent years has become a little pricy.

Pitlochry itself, with its Internationally renowned theatre and Victorian heritage, was located in what seemed like a sea of forests, lochs and hills. The hydroelectric scheme, which first brought electricity to the Highlands in the 1930s, was an additional attraction. This comprised of a dam with a built-in fish ladder. Salmon could use the fish ladder, a series of linked pools, to swim upriver and over the dam, to their spawning grounds. Visitors to the dam could see them in action through a viewing portal in one of the pools.

I was ready for a break when I arrived in the town at 10.10am and met up with Carmen & Alastair who had brought along Carmen's mum.

I pulled up at the Escape Route Café and Carmen came out to greet me. An embarrassing incident could have ensued at this point, but it was avoided. Let me explain...

Having to travel light I had only two of each item of clothing, so I adopted an on-bike clothes drying system. I would wash something, then tie it to the rack bag on the back of the bike where it would flap about in the wind for a few miles until it was dry. This turned out to be the most effective method of drying clothes. I was just glad it didn't rain, or I would have been stuck, unable to wash anything, and would probably have ended up very smelly.

So back to the Escape Route Café. Carmen came out to greet me and as she approached I remembered what item of clothing I had tied to the rack bag; it was a pair of blue and red striped underpants. I quickly stuffed them into my bag, and she didn't seem to have noticed them. I came clean later and she said she didn't see them, but I think perhaps she was just being kind!

They bought me a humungous cooked breakfast, a latte, and an equally huge Oat and Raisin Cookie for later, which set me up for the rest of the day's journey.

Travelling out of Pitlochry the gradient slowly increased past Killiecrankie, where you can see the Soldier's Leap; the spot where, in the seventeenth century, a Redcoat soldier leapt 18ft across the raging River Garry, fleeing the Jacobites. That's quite a leap, the length of three adults end on end. Mrs B and I had stopped here in the past and seeing the gap it must have been quite a feat.

Shortly Blair Atholl came into view, home of Blair Castle where Queen Victoria stayed in 1842, boosting the area's popularity.

After Blair Atholl, the road got steeper towards the Pass of Drumochter (Drumochter meaning 'high ridge') This was the main mountain pass between the northern and southern Scottish Highlands, which was used by the A9 road and the Highland Main Line, the railway between Inverness and the south of Scotland. The cycle path ran parallel to these mainly along the old A9.

A large warning sign at the bottom of the pass warned cyclists that 'Weather conditions can deteriorate without warning and can be severe even in summer – no food or shelter for 30km' A sobering thought, but there was no turning back at this point. This was the only way north from here without a huge diversion.

'Snoop, do you think we'll make it? I hope your survival training is up to date?'. I got a blank look.

The Drumochter Pass in winter is sometimes closed with snow gates on either side of the pass on the main A9 to stop traffic trying to brave the weather. Being the main route to Inverness, the road being closed would effectively cut off the north of Scotland from the south. Diverting in a car would involve heading to the east coast around the Cairngorms or heading west via Fort William and the Great Glen. Both diversions of hundreds of miles. On the bike? I don't think so!

I pressed on. Snow was very unlikely in September, and if I got into any kind of trouble, I wouldn't be far from the A9, and as such mobile coverage would be good. Plus Mrs B and several other people were following me on Polarsteps, tracking my every movement. So I could be pinpointed on a map should I need a rescue.

I had cycled this route before anyway and had driven over the pass numerous times, so I wasn't apprehensive about the prospect of the journey today. The cycle path itself on the old A9 was an easy gradient.

As I ascended the pass, the countryside changed from the fast-flowing River Garry and its tree-lined valley to more mountainous rocky terrain with a vista of moorland heather, and miles of scree-covered hillsides of epic proportions.

I paused at the Drumochter 1519-foot road summit and took in the view, the surrounding hills towering around me. At the end of the mountain range directly east of here, twenty-five miles as a crow might fly, was the

UK's highest mountain, Ben Nevis. Not able to be seen from here but so close.

The view was magnificent. The peace, fresh air, and sense of the vast expanse of space was something to experience. You can't get this in a car driving through, you have to be outside, in the wild and away from the buzz of cars and lorries.

It was all downhill for the next fifteen miles to Newtonmore! I had done this once before in 2013 when I cycled from Glasgow to Inverness, and it was brilliant. At the time I probably sat there with a silly smug smile on my face freewheeling down the hill.

I was hoping for a similar trip today, however, I could see rain ahead. The tell-tale streaky cloud touched the ground and it looked like my run of dry weather was coming to an end - I was going to get wet. I figured I had been blessed so far with good weather, and I was thankful for this. I mean, who could cycle the whole length of the country without getting wet? It would be almost impossible at any time of the year. I was prepared. Perhaps not prepared for constant heavy rain, but I was prepared for showers. Chef Snoopy had his cool blue waterproofs. I had my cycle jacket and waterproof trousers which were in practice waterproof-ish. My bags all had waterproof covers, so I checked all these were handy for when the time came.

I headed off towards the darkened skies, I was freewheeling, enjoying the ride, and in my bliss forgot about the possibility of an impending drenching.

After a few minutes, I noticed the clouds had lifted a little and I could see down the valley towards Dalwhinnie. I stopped to take in the view and the ground at my feet was wet, it had been raining here, but I hadn't been rained on yet. Did I cycle through the rain and not notice? Amazingly the rain clouds were now behind me along the path I'd just cycled. My mind was blown – I got an immediate sense that someone up there was looking after me on this journey.

Passing the whitewashed Dalwhinnie Distillery, I powered on towards my destination at Alvie, five miles short of Aviemore. It was getting late now and I calculated my arrival time at about 6.30pm, so I called the site, knowing that their office closed at 6pm.

'We'll leave your pitching instructions in the red box by the office door – we do this a lot'.

I breathed a sigh of relief. The brunch and snacks along the way were wearing off now, and I was getting tired, but the knowledge that I was nearly there spurred me on.

I arrived at Strathraddy Holiday Park just after 6.30pm, almost 12 hours after setting out in the morning. I had paid £10 for the night when I booked the pitch, and it was a large site.

I cycled into the site to the smell of barbequing. A posh, professional outdoor catering unit, the size of a large caravan, was onsite serving up lots of deliciously smelling food. A queue of people eagerly waited in line. I headed to the office and picked up my pitching instructions.

It was a holiday home and campervan site, with mostly static vans, but the camping field at the centre of the site was large and busy with over a dozen tents. I pitched up and thought about heading off to the posh-nosh van. I wondered if they did breakfasts. I toddled around and asked.

'No sorry, we don't open until lunchtime!'.

I was the only person there now, and it looked like they were packing up.

There are times when on the spur of the moment, my mind goes blank and later on I would wonder why I didn't react differently or ask another question. This was one of those times. Were they still serving? Did they have anything left? I turned and walked away disappointed that they didn't do breakfast. I should have turned back around, but for some odd reason didn't or couldn't. It doesn't make sense looking back on my reaction, but that's how it was.

Back at the tent, I sat on the picnic bench that I had pitched next to.

'Snoop, you're a chef. I'm sure you could cook me up a posh dinner. How about it?'

He wasn't committing to anything and was watching the other campers lighting their camping stoves and clinking their cooking tins.

I can't remember what I did eat that night, but it was likely another tin of cold Baked Beans. It made me more determined to find breakfast and a latte the next morning.

Back at my tent, I realised that my backside was no longer aching or painful. Mrs B had done it again. Removing the padding from the cycling shorts solved the problem. Who would have thought it?

I called Mrs B and updated her on my longest day so far, 82 miles. Tomorrow would be a little easier.

Miles of Memories

Day seventeen - Midgie mayhem

I woke up the next morning to the smell of fresh air & pine trees. I was in the Spey Valley. Speyside was very different from Perthshire on the other side of the Drumochter Pass. The ancient pine forests, peppered with lochs and lochans, home to wildlife such as red squirrels and the elusive capercaillie, were backed by the Cairngorm Mountains in a unique and ancient landscape.

I packed up quickly and headed towards Aviemore a few miles away.

Aviemore, the gateway to the Cairngorms National Park and all-year-round centre for outdoor activities, was a special place. Highlights were the Strathspey Steam Railway, the Cairngorm Funicular Railway – the highest mountain railway in the UK, and the Cairngorm Reindeer Centre, where you can meet and feed the herd as they roam the hillside.

My mission just now however was to get breakfast. Unfortunately, I forgot it was a Sunday and nowhere was open except the petrol station Wild Bean Café, a fast-food-on-the-go addition to the petrol station shop.

I got a bacon roll and a latte, which was adequate but a bit disappointing as I had visions of a full Scottish Breakfast in my head. I could sense Chef Snoopy disrespectfully sniggering, so I threw him a look.

'Cheeky article, you are'. I surprised myself by coming out with this phrase. Where it came from at this moment I've no idea, but I immediately pictured my mum. It was one of her sayings.

I often found myself coming out with phrases that she would have said. I guess they must have been ingrained into my memory. Mum had lots of her own phrases. She would often add 'tookles' to the end of words. Eggs would be 'eggytookles' but she also had another word for eggs: 'hoogies'. 'tosca-neenee' was toast, and 'wogawoga' – water, 'twaddle' - tea. Fortunately, she never strung these together into a sentence, which would have been just too confusing.

She had a comical way of dismissing you if she thought you were talking rubbish. 'fooey!' she would say. It wasn't a disbelieving 'Really?' But was more of a dismissive 'Don't talk rubbish!' or as they say in Scotland 'Aye right!'

Her kids would often be referred to endearingly as 'sausage' or 'chunky', and we just accepted it. Sometimes she would put on an exaggerated Lancashire accent:

'Ow do Chunky?'

I made the mistake of saying this to a female work colleague once. It didn't go down very well!

She's been gone several years now, and I can't remember all the words she made up, but I find occasionally another word comes back to me and I can hear her say it as if she were standing next to me.

'Today will be an easier day Snoop'

I tried to sound convincing. The route stats promised this, but I had let myself down before. 61 miles and one thousand feet less of an ascent compared to yesterday.

On my 2013 trip, the last leg of my journey was from Newtonmore to Inverness, which was also close to sixty miles, and along mostly the same roads. I do remember at the time being quite tired when arriving in Inverness. I was hoping that this time the journey from Land's End would indeed have boosted my fitness, so how I performed today would be a good measure.

Before leaving Aviemore we went on a trip down memory lane. It was here where we cooked for the kids' camp for 7 years. The actual camp was a mile or two from the town centre, but we would regularly run to Tesco in the main street to top up the food stock. It was hard work, but totally worth it.

'Do you remember this Snoop? We had some good times'

Snoop did remember and I could sense he was in deep thought reminiscing to himself.

Leaving Aviemore and heading north, again feeling like I could have stayed longer (or at least until somewhere opened for breakfast) put me in a contemplative mood about many of the places I had passed through on this journey. I guess the downside of a trip like this, in the timescale, is that you can't explore. You can only pass through. It would have been nice to spend more time in many of these transient places; experience the sights and sounds and take in the local culture. I felt a sadness that it was often hello and then goodbye in one breath to most of the locations.

We all need time to pause and ponder, and although that wasn't the aim of this trip, perhaps one day I could cycle LEJOG again, with more time to absorb the surroundings before moving on. One thing it was doing though, was helping me to build a list of places to revisit with Mrs B.

Heading to Carrbridge the incline rose and I stopped at the old packhorse bridge built in 1717, which formed a perfectly semi-circular arch over the river. Everyone stops here as it's rather photogenic. After being damaged in a major flood in 1829 which left it in its current state, it looked like it was held up by fresh air and wouldn't hold much weight these days.

Chef Snoopy wanted to run across it but I told him he'd break it. He's such a rebel sometimes...

Continuing uphill I arrived at the Slochd summit at 1500ft. (In pronunciation, the d becomes a t I believe) Again a gradual incline and it didn't seem like a lot of effort. Partly because the Aviemore area was already quite high at just under 1000ft. The train line ran over the summit alongside the cycle path, which again was on the old A9, and I paused to refuel, and maybe spot the Highland Express heading down to, or coming up from, Inverness.

'It's all downhill to Inverness now Snoop'. However, Chef Snoopy had other things on his mind and was looking a little apprehensive. I then realised we weren't alone. The midges had spotted us and we were attracting them like iron filings to a magnet.

The Scottish Midge, looking like tiny mosquitoes, were world-famous for bringing terror to campers and outdoor enthusiasts. Swarming in their hundreds and thousands they could be a real pest. Fortunately, they don't carry diseases as mosquitos do, but they still bite. Up to this point I hadn't encountered any midges, possibly because they are worse in more north and west regions, and I'd been travelling up the centre of Scotland. But they appeared in force at the Slochd summit.

The longer we stood, the more midges we were attracting. The word was obviously getting around in the midge world.

'human flesh – come and get it!'

Snoop hid in my rucksack, and I could feel their tiny bites on my neck, arms, and legs. Generally, I'm fortunate in that my body doesn't react to the bites and come out in red spots, but midges are nonetheless irritating. I moved on quickly leaving them behind waiting for their next victim.

As I cycled down towards Inverness, I was again looking for diversions to cut down my journey mileage. NCN7 near Inverness does a loop out to the east through Culloden, so I thought about bypassing this with a more direct road, however, I missed the turn-off and ended up completing the loop after all.

This route took me past the Clava Cairns, a group of three Bronze Age circular chamber tomb cairns. Basically, an intriguing 4,000-year-old graveyard, which was scouted as one of the filming locations for the popular Outlander television series.

The three cairns were well-preserved, each having a central chamber. Two of the cairns had entrance passages, while the chamber of the central cairn was enclosed. Each cairn surrounded by a ring of standing stones. Fifty cairns of this type could be found in the area around Inverness.

Arriving in Inverness, capital of the Highlands, which achieved city status in the year 2000, I knew I only had 15 more miles to go today. I rolled into the city centre and parked up at Costa, with its outside seating. It was strange, but I didn't feel I needed to be as security conscious as in other cities, however, one eye was still on the bike as I ordered at the counter.

The last few miles today were into unfamiliar territory. I hadn't ventured north beyond Inverness for several years. In fact, I think the last time was in the 1980s when journeying north-west to Ullapool and over to the islands of Lewis and Harris. This time I would be heading in a different direction; north through Dingwall; I had not ventured this far northeast before, and I was looking forward to the prospect of seeing new places.

I headed off across the Kessock Bridge into the north Highlands. After the central route up the country to reach Inverness, the route now followed the east coast around the inlets and firths of Cromarty, Moray, and Beauly, crossing the Black Isle, which wasn't an island but a peninsula almost surrounded by the three firths. Accessed by ferry in the past, the Black Isle would have been pretty much like visiting an island.

After crossing the peninsular I headed down to Dingwall at the head of the Cromarty Firth. I made good time today and arrived at 4.30pm. I couldn't believe it and did a double-take to see if I'd seen the time wrong. Dingwall had a good feel to it.

I noticed quite a few impressive-looking buildings. The town must have been an important hub at one time. This was indeed the case; Dingwall was once the administrative centre for the north Highlands.

The history of the town however dated much further back to the Vikings and grew from these Nordic beginnings to become a significant port, with a harbour built by none other than Thomas Telford in about 1820. That Telford guy certainly got about. Unfortunately, little evidence of Dingwall's maritime history now remained.

I received a very warm welcome at the Dingwall Camping & Caravanning Club site. The site manager Marion greeted me, spotting I was a cycling backpacker, and immediately told me they owed me money. I must have looked a bit baffled, so she clarified,

'Booking on the website doesn't give you a backpacker option, so you've paid too much'.

I paid £16 online for the pitch tonight.

'Leave it with me love, and I'll refund you £8'.

Brilliant! I thanked her very much, she didn't need to do this, but she did.

I spotted that her accent was from the Midlands and mentioned that my dad came from West Bromwich.

'How did you end up here in Dingwall?' I asked.

'We managed a site down south and this opportunity came up, so we moved. We love it here!'

This was another site with lots of camper vans, and it dawned on me that the attraction here must be the North Coast 500.

I was given a nicely mown pitch on the edge of the site and set up my tent. It was a lovely site and very clean.

I reflected on my journey today, having covered a few more miles than my trip from Newtonmore to Inverness in 2013, and a higher total elevation, but I felt great. Hardly tired at all. The comparison was useful. It showed that at this point I was fitter than I was 8 years previously. Cycling almost every day for the previous 16 days had obviously boosted my fitness quite a bit. I was on top of the world.

Tonight I had a dinner date with friends Cher & Richard, who lived close to Inverness, but they weren't around when I cycled through the city. They kindly chose to drive up to Dingwall to take me to a local Indian restaurant.

I got myself cleaned up as best as I could and headed out to Café India where they bought dinner and we had a good catch-up recalling some of my adventures so far.

I have to say that I was so thankful for all the friends who supported me along the way, not only in person but on Facebook and the Polarsteps app. It would have been a very lonely venture without everyone's support and encouragement.

I bid Cher & Richard goodbye and headed back to my tent for a good night's sleep on a full stomach. Little did I know a major dilemma would be waiting for me in the morning.

Alan Loach

Day eighteen - Dilemma in Dingwall

'Snoop we have a problem. A big problem...'

It wasn't a good start to the day, and today was one of those unavoidable marathon days where campsite availability didn't line up with my plans.

At the planning stage, this part of the route proved to be a bit of an issue; the next 90 miles were the remotest of the whole trip, with few places to camp that I could find.

I thought about wild camping at one stage and possibly camping at the remote settlement of Altnaharra, but there didn't appear to be a campsite here. I couldn't quite make the combination of sixty miles and available campsites fit. Wild camping didn't appeal. I would rather have access to a proper toilet, and the uncertainty of camping somewhere I shouldn't be would have made for a restless night's sleep. So today was potentially 89 miles!

I woke early to get a head start. The plan was to leave at 7.30am and allow eleven and a half hours for the trip to

Tongue, so arriving about 7pm. The Tongue campsite office closed at 8pm so I had a little leeway.

I packed up the tent, packed everything onto the bike, and noticed that my saddle was a bit loose.

'What's going on here Snoop?'

I thought initially that one of the bolts had loosened but looking underneath the saddle I could see that one of the two rails that supported the saddle had snapped. A moment of panic! This couldn't have happened on a worse day. I stood for a while in disbelief. I can't abandon my cycle now, being so close to the finish line. I took off my panic hat and put on my logic hat. Choices, what were my choices?

'Snoop I need some ideas here. What do you think?' He was in deep thought.

The bike might have been rideable as it was, but how far would I get? The second support would be under pressure and would probably snap too under the strain. Cycling 90 miles in the standing position didn't even bear thinking about. Did I have anything to repair the broken support with? Tesco was open, I could buy some glue or tape, or something?...... No these wouldn't hold.

My dad's way of fixing things crossed my mind. His fixes for things were, shall we say, unique. His talent for such things came from serving as a camp cook in the Second World War in Burma and having to improvise with what was at hand.

When he had the hotel in the 1980s, the sun lounge roof was leaking. Dad would be up on the roof with some pastry, obviously industrial strength pastry, but pastry nonetheless, to fix it. What was in that pastry I've no idea, but it was one of those things that seemed to have a multitude of uses. Unfortunately, I didn't have any of Dad's pastry today, and I wouldn't have been convinced that it would fix this specific issue anyway.

I had tie-wraps in my toolkit. Could I use these to somehow secure the saddle? I inspected the break and tried to find a way of attaching the tie-wrap so that it would support the saddle.... this wasn't going to work.

There was a bike shop in Dingwall, when would it open?

'Snoop when does the bike shop open?' He didn't know.

I asked Mr Google in desperation. It opened at 9am but I needed to get going. Would they have saddles anyway? It was only a small shop, but surely they would have a saddle or some way of repairing the one I had? It was 7.15am. If I waited for the shop to open, I would be two hours behind on my already tight schedule.

I weighed up the options, there was no way I could ride another three days on a broken saddle. I still had almost 200 miles to cycle, and if it snapped completely in the middle of nowhere I would be really up the creek without a paddle (or a saddle in my case). A temporary repair wasn't going to last. So I decided to wait for the bike shop to open.

'Well, Snoop I'm going to need your help today. I'm looking for inspiration here!'. I could see he was thinking about it in silent contemplation, but he came up with nothing.

In the meantime, I resigned myself to waiting. Batty's Baps, an early morning café on the Dingwall high street, was open and I had a breakfast bap and a latte. So the day got off to a good start in one way at least, and I contemplated how I was going to make the rest of the day work.

The cycle shop opened at 9am, and I was hoping someone might be there a little earlier. At 8.40 I was outside the shop front waiting and watching as people approached, hoping they were there to open up, only for them to walk by to another destination. I paced up and down like a caged animal, then finally a guy on a bike arrived at 8.45 and I wondered if he was a potential customer or an employee. He didn't look me in the eye, but I wasn't in the mood to wait for an opportunity to speak to him, and got straight to the point,

'Hello, are you here to open up?'. He kept his head down and replied

'We don't open until 9am'.

It sounded like he'd got out of bed on the wrong side this morning. I guess it was Monday morning after all, so I didn't ask any more questions. He proceeded to open up and started bringing bikes out of the shop to form a pavement display ignoring me completely. Another couple of employees arrived and one of them was friendly enough to inform me they had to get all the bikes out to make room in the shop to serve me. Fair enough.

I was asked inside at about 9.05 and by 9.20 had a new saddle on my bike and I headed off. I was 2 hours behind on my schedule and options were still running through my head.

After an hour of cycling and thinking through the limited possibilities for getting to Tongue before the campsite office closed, I arrived in Alness.

I had spotted on Google that there was a good bakers shop here, the Harry Gow Bakery, so I stopped for a latte and also bought a nice ham salad roll for lunch later. I sat on a bench outside with my latte.

'Where are you off to today?'. A guy sitting on the next bench enquired.

'Tongue hopefully,' I said, and a wave of doubt crossed my mind. His jaw dropped to the floor.

'Today?' he said with an expression of disbelief on his face. 'The nights are drawing in'.

I responded by saying I did have lights for the bike. But then I thought, with 80 miles to go and the last 35 miles of this over remote moorland, I could be in the middle of the moors when it got dark. Now I've seen movies where people get caught out on the moors as it goes dark, and it doesn't usually turn out very well at all.

This called for drastic action. What was I doing just sitting here?

I had a choice at Alness. My planned route followed the coast at a low level, heading out to the east and then turning northwest: this was the low road. There was another route over the hill directly north from Alness, which was ten miles shorter, but this road rose to almost 1000ft: this was the high road.

It wasn't a difficult choice; I chose the high road. After all, 'The hills are my friends'. This was Struie Road, and it wasn't too bad in terms of the gradient. No getting off to push today – no time for that nonsense. The views of the Dornoch Firth and its surroundings were stunning from the top.

Once over the hill, I was back on my planned route. The diversion paid off, cutting an hour from my journey time. I must admit though, even with this saving I knew I had to pedal like crazy to make up the time.

I stopped for a breather after the challenge of the hill.

'Morning – are you OK?', a passing cycling called over to me – it was Campsite Girl. What? Where did she come from? I last saw her in the Forest of Bowland, she was faster than me, and I had a day off, but she was still behind me! What's going on here?

'Yes I'm good, thank you'. She didn't stop and was gone, disappearing around a bend in the road. I continued myself and stopped again for lunch shortly afterwards in Ardgay where there was a nice bench and nearby toilets. The salad roll from Harry Gow's Bakery was truly delicious, note-to-self to visit this baker's shop again.

My route continued north on good roads until I was directed by Komoot onto an unexpected route diversion down a narrow unkempt track. Thinking this must be a mistake, I checked the Sustrans route. The route was correct. This was NCN1. It led to the Shin Railway Viaduct

A metal-framed footbridge bolted onto the side of the sandstone viaduct allowed pedestrians and bikes to cross. But the steps on the bridge didn't allow easy passage across. I carried my bike down the steps thinking that I definitely wouldn't be taking this route next time.

'Snoop, I think Sustrans are having a laugh here!'

The roads were very quiet around here, so this would be another reroute should I do LEJOG again

The viaduct itself traversed the Kyle of Sutherland, a water inlet linked to the Dornoch Firth, allowing the passage of trains to the far north, Wick and Thurso. I realised that I would pass over here on the train back to Inverness in a few days.

Once over the bridge, I joined up with the A836 and followed the River Shin to the peaceful village of Lairg, known as the crossroads of the north, as several roads north, south, east, and west converged here. The Inverness to Thurso train also stopped here. This would be my last glimpse of civilisation for a few hours. Soon I would see the last of the trees and head onto the moorland.

Three miles north of Lairg I screeched to a halt. A road sign confirmed the distance over the stretch of moorland I had to cross: Tongue 35 miles. I stared at the roadsign and considered the crossing, which was one of the remotest and most hostile areas in the UK. A thought crossed my mind: could I survive with no phone signal and no mobile data? I laughed out loud at the thought. What did we all do before mobile phones? Just 30 years ago, nobody had a mobile phone. Probably because they were like bricks, required a two-foot ariel to work, and a separate huge battery pack. Not to mention the cost and next to no coverage.

Where was my faith? Was it in a mobile phone? I didn't think so. I was heading into the unknown, but I wasn't doing it alone. With renewed confidence, I pushed on.

'Here we go then Snoop. Hope we make it before it gets dark'.

I wasn't confident about getting to Tongue before the campsite office closed and thought it might be a good idea to contact them while I had a phone signal in case I arrived after 8pm.

'Call me if you arrive after 8pm and I'll come down and book you in'. Mick the campsite manager assured me. I guess he must have received calls like mine all the time.

The moorland I was entering was called The Flow Country which covered Caithness and Sutherland in the far north of Scotland. This was a vast expanse of blanket peat bog comprising of a complex set of interlinked pools that hosted amazing plants and rare birds. The flora and fauna here apparently played a vital role in our defence against the effects of climate change.

As I cycled along the narrow single-carriageway road; a causeway that seemed to float over the wetlands, the solitude and silence were very noticeable. The occasional car or van passed by, but the peace and tranquillity in this place was almost tangible. There was nothing for miles and miles except peat bog and distant mountains, but the landscape was far from boring or dull. A couple of times I stopped and breathed in the peace of my surroundings.

After a while, the road dipped into a valley and the settlement of Altnaharra.

There was a hotel and a scattering of houses, two abandoned petrol pumps, and a view of what I named 'Half-eaten Mountain'. It looked like a local giant had taken a bite out of it. The place looked idyllic, a haven in the wilderness. But then this was the last flourish of summer, and it probably wouldn't be as inviting, or accessible, in the winter months. I was halfway over the moorland.

Continuing, the road rose again to almost 1000ft and then dropped to the shores of Loch Loyal and Loch Craggie, and I knew I was on the final stretch. After the lochs was a final climb before the drop into Tongue. I stopped at the top of the climb for a few minutes to take in the view as the sun hung low in the sky, and a cyclist appeared behind me. You guessed it, it was Campsite Girl again.

'Wait a minute,' I said. 'How come you keep passing me, but you're always behind me?'. I think she was as surprised as I was. I mentioned she passed me earlier in the day.

'Oh was that you? I didn't realise!' she said. 'It's unusual to keep meeting the same person along a route'

I don't know if she was looking for some meaning why we kept bumping into each other, but I wasn't. It was just rather odd. We finally exchanged names, her name was Claire, and she suddenly became very friendly and suggested we cycle the remaining two miles down the hill to Tongue together. So we did.

We arrived at the campsite at 6.15pm and I was amazed at how quickly I had completed the cycle. I hadn't been checking the time or my progress along the way, but watching the sun as it began to fall towards the horizon. I just got my head down and was pedalling like there was no tomorrow.

The Tongue Campsite was right on the shore and consisted of a 36-bed hostel surrounded by caravan, motorhome, and tent pitches. Surrounding it the scenery in Tongue was amazing, with imposing mountains and deep sea lochs.

Claire went into the main house to check in and I stayed outside watching her bike. Likewise, when she came out I went in.

'Shall we go and find a pitch?'. I thought wait a minute; she thinks I'm her best buddy now. Snoop gave me his best evil, unblinking, stare. I got the message.

I pitched my tent next to Claire's thinking this was too close for comfort, but I didn't want to offend her.

'I'm staying at John O'Groats tomorrow and taking the ferry to Orkney the next day to stay a night at a friend's. Do you want to come?'.

I was a bit surprised by the question. I really didn't want to divert from my plan to stay in Thurso tomorrow night. Not that I was averse to last-minute changes and replanning – I'd done this with my route quite a few times. This just didn't feel right. I had booked Thurso for two nights, and in any case, what would Mrs B think about me taking off to Orkney with someone half my age? It wasn't even a consideration. However, I didn't think for a minute that she had anything other than company on her mind.

I hesitated to respond, not wanting to appear even more antisocial than I already seemed.

'Sounds like an idea – appreciate the offer. I'll think about it,'. I said eventually. But inside I was saying 'No way!'

The light was failing by the time I settled and I heard Claire lighting her cooking stove and clanking her cooking utensils. I sat in my tent and stared at my tin of cold beans. Warm beans might have been nice for a change, or even hot beans, with perhaps some cheese melted over the top. I would have died for beans on buttered toast. Real butter of course. Or perhaps chips and beans. Chilli Beans were good too, nice and spicy. But I was getting a bit carried away now and realised I was drooling.

In any case, going outside on a warm windless Scottish summer, almost autumn, evening in this part of Scotland was not a good idea. The midges were now out in force and everyone had retreated to their own tents. Beans with a side of midges? Maybe not.

Day nineteen - NC500 to Thurso

The penultimate day! Penultimate - one of those words that to me doesn't sound right. Another word that comes to mind is 'raze' as in 'raze to the ground'. If you raze (as in raise) something, does it not go in an upward direction? I wonder who makes these words up. Confusing.

Anyway – the second last day had arrived. I woke to a stunning dawn in Tongue. The name Tongue was said to come from the old Norse word 'tunga', a tongue of land that projected into the loch.

The Vikings, some say, occupied the area between 800AD and 1200AD. No evidence of their presence remained. However, it's believed that the now ruined Castle Varrich, also known as Caisteal Bharraigh, overlooking the Kyle of Tongue, was built around this time.

The long challenging cycles were done, and I was on the home straight! Lots of people were up and about this morning, including Claire. I found out she worked for some kind of media production company and was from Birmingham, but she didn't have a Midlands accent.

'I've travelled around the country a bit and lost my accent'.

I broke the news that I had decided to stick to my plans and not go to Orkney but thanked her again for the offer.

The sun was out today so I reached for my sunglasses, but I couldn't find them. What had I done with them? Did I roll them in the tent as I did before? I unpacked everything and still couldn't find them. People were leaving now and Claire was standing around, perhaps waiting for me. I did a second search of all my belongings, but they were nowhere to be found.

'Snoop where could they be?' He had no idea. 'You're supposed to know these things as my co-rider!'.

I thought about where I might have last had them... Cycling into the campsite yesterday, I had them on... Then I went into the booking office... It was dark in there... Ah! I probably took them off in there. I concluded I must have put them down on the desk in the office when paying the site fees and not picked them back up.

I walked around to the office: 'Office opens at 9.30am' it said on the door. It was 8.30am. I went back around to the bike and told Claire I would need to hang about for an hour. She decided to head off. I waited. I only had forty miles to cycle today, so I didn't need to rush.

The views were lovely and the morning sun bathed the hills in an orange glow. The water on the Kyle of Tongue inlet was so calm, and people were working on some kind of fish or shellfish farm just off the rugged shore. The causeway across the Kyle, partly the natural 'tongue' part of the landscape and partly man-made, carried cars, bikes and campers from one side to the other. Another link in the NC500.

I was on the lookout for someone approaching the office before 9.30am and decided to put my helmet on, which was hanging from the handlebars, so I was ready to head off once I'd retrieved my glasses. As I turned the helmet over, my sunglasses fell out. Doh!

I must admit to losing things around the house. Although we don't have a very big house, I'm always losing my glasses, my phone, and my keys. Every time I waste so much time looking for them, I promise myself that I'm going to put them down in the same place every time in future, so I'll know where they are. Do I do this – no!

I popped my glasses on and we were off once again.

Having only half the distance of yesterday to cover and being slightly stiff from the previous day's 80-mile trek, I intended to have a leisurely cycle to Thurso.

I set off and joined the NC500 route east; initially a single-carriageway road with passing places. It was campervan and motorbike land up there, and a bit like the dodgems. Some people had no concept of what passing places were for, and others in their impatience brushed past me very close.

The NC500 had become very popular as a staycation (a word which was once used for a holiday staying at home, but now seems to mean staying in the UK). This destination had much appeal during the pandemic for lots of reasons; it was a long way from the COVID hotspots, you could isolate in a camper van, and you didn't have to get there in an airborne sardine can. Understandable, but the roads up here weren't designed to take this volume of traffic, and I'd heard a few stories of locals getting a little upset.

My first mission was to find a caffeine top-up. This was hardly Costa or Starbucks land, so I knew I had a task at hand. Google Maps revealed a café at Bettyhill Tourist Information Centre, so I pushed on hoping for a result. I arrived at Bettyhill, which *was* actually on a hill, at about 10.45.

From what I could see from the main road, it comprised of clusters of houses, a small hotel and shop, a caravan park, a school and a church. All on a headland with two bays, amazing views, and lovely unspoiled golden beaches.

I pulled up to the Clachan Café at the Information Centre. 'Closed,' it said on the door. The opening times were displayed on another sign, and it looked like they opened at 11am. OK, 15 minutes to go….

'Hello again'. A familiar voice. I turned around.

'Sorry I didn't see you there'. Claire was sitting on a picnic bench just beyond the Centre.

'You waiting for coffee?'

'Yup!'

I sat opposite her and chatted for a few minutes. She'd previously mentioned doing 100km a day and I wondered why she planned in kilometres. She did give me a reason, but I must have been in a badly decaffeinated state as I couldn't remember her answer. I think it had something to do with an ex-boyfriend.

A couple of ladies of retirement age arrived at 11am, opened up and quickly put on a flask of filter coffee. I wondered if one was called Betty and did she live up the hill? I thought it wise not to ask. We queued up and got a cup of filter coffee with cold milk. Not quite a latte, but importantly it had caffeine in it. There wasn't much on offer in the way of anything else, so we sat on the picnic bench watching others coming and going.

Another cyclist pulled up. This was the last day of his two-week LEJOG.

'The weather's been amazing, only one really wet day...'

I tried not to feel too smug about missing this rainy day during my 'day off'. He had all the gear and was younger and fitter than me. His girlfriend was picking him up at John O'Groats that afternoon.

Then a whole bunch of Lycra-clad middle-aged guys screamed in from the Thurso direction followed by two support vans. I say screamed, as they were very loud and the tranquillity of the village was shattered. One was shouting into his mobile phone, obviously not getting a good signal, and thinking that shouting at the top of his voice was going to make a difference. I wonder what Betty would have to say about this?

'Aye townies, comin' oot here with their fancy dress and technology.'

They took over the Info Centre car park and I felt it was time to move on. Claire must have had the same thought as me about the noisy arrivals, and she decided it was time to press on too.

'I'm just going to finish my coffee. Maybe see you later if you stop again?' I said, thinking selfishly that I probably wasn't going to see her again. I caught a glimpse of a sheep shaking its head in the adjacent field as if it could read my thoughts.

Thankfully, the noisy Lycra guys would be heading in the opposite direction to me, so I finished off my coffee and set off again towards Thurso.

The road meandered with long curved stretches, hugging the coast and rising and falling with the headlands and the valley crossings. Some of these downhills were very exhilarating. It was easy to see why motorcyclists loved this route.

There was a cool breeze today, and the wind on my face as I picked up speed made my eyes stream, making it difficult to see the way ahead. I was so glad there were no sheep on the road to collide with.

Now there's a thought. What would happen if I collided with a sheep? (not that I would want to hurt a sheep) Would I bounce off the dense woolly coat? I mean it wouldn't be the same as colliding with a cow. That would probably produce a similar effect as doing a bellyflop. That would hurt. I'm sure there must be a farmer out there who knows the answer, but not something I would recommend or want to try.

Nearing Thurso, I got my first view of Orkney over the water. Amazing! I must be getting close.

I hadn't been this far north before, and I must admit that the countryside was not what I was expecting. I had visions of it being much more barren than it was, a perpetual moorland with rocky outcrops to the shoreline. But no, the land up here was arable, there were trees, gardens, ploughed fields, farms, and livestock. I thought about this and asked myself what I expected. I think I had fallen into the north / south mindset that many people do, which seems to get worse the further south you live. I know people from the south of England who think the whole of Scotland is covered in snow and ice for a large part of the winter. Whereas, in reality, most lower-lying areas of Scotland see none or very little snow in the winter. I guess that living in the south of Scotland, I must have had the same mindset about the north. Yes, it's remote, and generally a few degrees colder than further south, but it wasn't the bleak moorland that I imagined.

Thurso appeared on the horizon, mainland Scotland's most northerly town, and home to the country's most northerly railway station. It was only about 3pm. After yesterday's marathon, I felt like I'd only just started the cycle. I had already looked up places to eat for tonight and I spotted Robin's Fish & Chips on the way through the town as I made my way to my destination.

The campsite was perched on the cliffs beyond the town centre and had magnificent views of Orkney. There seemed to be plenty of space, but it was early in the day. I guessed that NC500 travellers would arrive about tea-time and fill the site up a little.

The site office was in a disused (because of Covid) café area manned by a young guy who must have seen so many people coming and going, he was very scripted. I got off to a bad start by forgetting to put my face mask on when entering the building.

'Mask please' he ordered.

Mask on and I said I'd booked for two nights. He looked me up in his paper diary and then I threw him off-script.

'Would it be possible to have an electric hook-up for one night?'

He explained that the electric pitch was in a different location to the non-electric pitches so I would have to move after one night.

'Not a problem,' I said,

I guess that made sense, but I had obviously thrown him into confusion with the request as he only charged me for one night.

'I think I owe you more money than this' I suggested.

He quickly changed the amount without much feedback or emotion.

I guessed that the lad must have been new to the job.

I found the electric pitch and put up the tent to find a tent peg missing. I needed six for the tent base and four for the guy ropes. I only had nine.

'Snoop, you haven't hidden a tent peg have you?' I looked him in the eye and he was a picture of innocence, but I knew better. He didn't respond.

'Well if you haven't got it, I must have lost it at Tongue'.

I briefly considered my options but decided that because the weather was very calm, three guy ropes would be sufficient for the last two nights.

It was still mid-afternoon and I knew all the hard work to get this far had been done. I was feeling such a sense of peace and calm as I knew that tomorrow was a short cycle to the finish line. I could have made it to John O'Groats today, but I was glad I chose to hold off so I could really enjoy tomorrow and spend some time at John O'Groats without having a deadline to get back.

I stocked up in the local Lidl, bought a delicious cod and chips at Robin's and checked in with Mrs B.

I was hoping for a good night's sleep to be ready for the last day.

'Goodnight Snoop, we're nearly there!'

Alan Loach

Day twenty - Hello John O'Groats

I was almost there. Twenty miles to John O'Groats, I could hardly believe it.

My train to Inverness was booked for tomorrow; I had booked it some time ago. But booking the train back from Thurso was a little more complicated than I expected. Scotrail allows you to book your bike along with your train ticket, but even though I tried booking well in advance, none of the trains on my original finish day, or the day after, had bike spaces.

It was early July when I phoned Scotrail Customer Care to see what they might advise.

'I'm hoping to travel on the 16th of September from Thurso to Croy, and I need a bike space,' I asked.

Croy station was close to home so this would be ideal. The lady on the phone checked on the 16th

'Sorry, no spaces on the 16th'.

'How about the 17th'?

'Sorry, no spaces on the 17th'.

I thought for a few seconds. If I could at least get down to Inverness I would have more choice of transportation for the rest of the journey, and Mrs B could even pick me up from there. But I got the same response.

'Sorry, no spaces on the 16th or 17th to Inverness'. 'There are only three services a day from Thurso, and lots of cyclists do North Coast 500 taking the train south from Thurso,' she said. 'It's getting very popular you know'.

'Do you get cancellations at all?' I asked in desperation. She didn't confirm.

'Try calling back nearer the time' she advised.

I think she was getting a little impatient with me asking her to check out different times, days and routes, so I thanked her and hung up.

I was thinking about what she was saying about cyclists doing the North Coast 500. It didn't quite make sense. The NC500 is a circular route. If cyclists took the train home from Thurso, then they must have started and finished at Thurso. Assuming that the majority of people doing the NC500 would be from south of Inverness, why would a cyclist travel to the most northerly point to start the route? Perhaps some cyclists do a partial

NC500 and travel back from Thurso? Anyway, I had to work out a plan B.

Plan B boiled down to a choice between getting the bike couriered to Inverness and taking the train without the bike or cycling back to Inverness down the coast road. I had two spare days after finishing LEJOG, so decided to cycle back to Inverness. I could do this in two days, and Mrs B agreed to pick me up from Inverness in the car. I did however keep an eye on the Scotrail website. Not with much hope, I had to admit, but I looked.

Then one day in early August I checked the Scotrail website again and found a bike space on the midday train the day after I would finish the cycle. I was elated and booked it immediately.

This worked out perfectly. I would stay two nights in Thurso, as I did in Penzance and cycle to John O'Groats and back in one day. The next day I would get the train to Inverness and be reunited with Mrs B.

So there was no rush today. I got up late, had a leisurely stroll along Thurso seafront and had a full breakfast and a latte at Derya's Cafe watching the surfers in the bay. You might have thought I would be desperate to get to John O'Groats, but no, I was chilling. I could get there in two hours, so I had all day. Much like at Penzance, I could leave many of my belongings in the tent and travel a little lighter today – an added bonus.

After breakfast, I headed back to the campsite to move my tent to the non-electric area, which was a short distance from where I camped the previous night. The middle of this area was occupied by a group of bikers, motorbikers that is, who had arranged their tents in a circle with a campfire in the middle. They were just packing up.

I spotted a nice pitch near a fenced-off area to which I could lock the bike and started to unpack my stuff. I threw my tent on the ground, about to unpack it, and was amazed to find a single tent peg on the grass.

'Where did that come from Snoop?' He was as perplexed as I was.

'Did you put it there?' I said accusingly. His expression didn't change. He was so good at keeping a straight face.

There was no sign of any tents having been in the immediate vicinity, and as it turned out, the peg was of a slightly different design to the tent pegs I had.

'Well Snoop, I guess we now have a full set of tent pegs again. The big guy's looking after us!'

I pitched the tent, totally amazed at the favour we'd had on this amazing adventure.

Shortly, the tent was back up, my excess baggage inside, and I was heading through Thurso and eastwards towards John O'Groats.

The skies were a little grey and the forecast held the possibility of rain, but I had come this far without getting wet. The main thing was to get to the finish line, it didn't matter what the weather did now.

The cycle route headed inland on farm roads. The main volume of traffic took the coast road, so I had the road almost to myself.

As I cycled, I could see mist hugging the coastline and a foghorn in the distance blasted out a warning to the shipping. I wondered if it was going to be foggy at John O'Groats.

The route skimmed Castletown Harbour, and Dunnet Bay through the remnants of an industrial past of flagstone quarrying, before heading back inland. Houses and farms dotted the largely flat landscape. Small settlements of a few houses and a school came and went.

As I approached my journey's end, I passed John O'Groats fire station, which looked like a large residential garage, then a coastguard station, another garage-type building. The sign for the junction ahead said: 'John O'Groats A99'. It pointed left.

I was at the very last double-digit A-road in the country! At the junction were the Seaview Hotel, Caberfeidh Bed & Breakfast, and a handful of bungalows. The village filling station, shop, and post office (all in one building) were to the right. But there were cottages dotted over a larger area. I turned left to the harbour.

The sense of excitement had been building as I cycled, and I was now bursting with a multitude of senses: joy, relief, achievement, and disbelief that I had done it, to name a few. I must have been grinning from ear to ear as I rolled into John O'Groats harbour. Check me! I had just cycled the whole length of the country! I clocked the total at 1163 miles.

My journey was perhaps against the odds in many ways. I had some struggles but had been blessed on several aspects of the trip. It could have been so much more difficult. The weather: I had no rain and didn't get wet once, and the temperature stayed about 19 degrees for the whole trip, a perfect cycling temperature. No punctures: the bike took every type of terrain in its stride. All my struggles of the last three weeks had evaporated.

I found a seat and just stared at the John O'Groats signpost for I don't know how long. Did I just dream all this? Was it real? Will I suddenly sit bolt upright in bed at home with Chef Snoopy staring at me on the bedside table with a mocking look on his face? No, this was real, and it was sinking in. Every turn of the pedals, every ache and pain, and every moment of discomfort didn't matter anymore. I would go through it all again for the elation that I felt on that day.

It was still misty, but dry, with the occasional glimpse of the sun. There was no wind and the rippling waves gently lapped the rocks along the shore. I concluded that I liked John O'Groats.

Mrs B had been here years ago before we met.

'There's nothing there!' she told me.

There probably wasn't then, but there was now. Not over commercialised, there was a nice little harbour, places to buy ice cream, fish & chips, a small discreet souvenir shop, and a coffee shop.

'So Snoop, who exactly was this John O'Groats chap?' I knew he wouldn't know, but I waited for an answer. As usual, he just sat there as if he hadn't heard a word I said.

It's said that the settlement of John O' Groats was named after a Dutchman, Jan de Groot.

In 1496 the islands of Orkney had just been won from Norway by King James IV and we're now under Scottish rule. To service the islands De Groot was granted a licence to operate the 6-mile ferry route.

I found out later that two miles to the west of here De Groot's gravestone, known as the John De Groat Stone, could be seen in the vestibule of Canisbay Kirk. I had cycled through the hamlet of Canisbay and right past this church and would cycle past it again on the way back to Thurso, not knowing these facts. Ah, the benefits of hindsight!

People milled about from place to place, taking photos next to the signpost (no commercial photographers to be seen). Some had arrived on foot, some on bikes or motorbikes, but most people were in cars and camper vans.

I called Mrs B, 'I made it!'

'I'm so proud of you! Everyone's so proud of you. Well done!'

'Chef Snoopy would like a word'. I held the phone to his ear, but he was characteristically silent, off in a world of his own.

'He's having a quiet moment to himself' I explained

We chatted for a while.

I bought a latte and took a few photos just as the sun burst out and the mist lifted. Orkney appeared out of the mist, six miles away over the water. I still wasn't tempted to hop on the boat, but Mrs B and I will likely do this one day. I was a happy camper.

'Excuse me!'

I turned around and a lady with a dog was standing behind me.

'Have you cycled from Land's End?'.

'I have!' Just saying it, I couldn't believe it. 'I really have!'.

'That's amazing. Well done!'

The clue was on my cycle shirt emblazoned with 'LAND'S END TO JOHN O'GROATS

'Would you like me to take some photos for you next to the sign?'

'That's very kind. Thank you!'

I picked up Snoop and left the bike to one side.

'Don't you want a photo with the bike'

'No just me and my co-rider

It was traditional at John O'Groats to pick up your bike and hold it aloft, over your head in victory, for the final photo.

'There's no way I'm picking up that bike' I thought.

OK, I probably could have or should have. But being a tourer, and a little tougher than the average bike, it was quite heavy. Besides if I'd picked up the bike, how would Snoop get in the photo? I couldn't leave him out, he'd be furious!

She took several photos of myself and Snoop. I thanked her and she was on her way. They turned out much better than the selfie I had planned.

I watched the gulls hovering on the air currents. Guillemots, fulmars, oystercatchers, and kittiwakes could be seen around here, as well as Atlantic puffins. I had read that the area around John O'Groats was one of the best places in the UK to see them. I didn't see any puffins though as the best time was during their breeding season of May to early July.

I spent almost 3 hours just chilling, people-watching. I didn't want this day to end. Returning to Thurso, my bike seemed to float on air, and I didn't have a care in the world.

Alan Loach

Alan Loach

Next time - If I did it again….

I posted these words on my blog to cries of disbelief, but it was my way of debriefing. My mission had been accomplished, and as with all good trips, a personal debrief happened in my head over the next few days. What went well? What didn't go so well? What did I get out of it? What could I pass on to those who might want to do it themselves?

The advice below is from my personal experience and your experience or needs may be very different, but here goes…

The route.

I chose the National Cycle Network to travel on after being inspired by the Sustrans book. Firstly I must say that I didn't follow the book to the letter. It split the journey into 28 sections, therefore 4 weeks of cycling to reach John O'Groats. Some of the sections I thought were very short for a day's cycle, the shortest being 20 miles, so I simply took the 1200-mile route and shoehorned it into 3 weeks, giving me an average of 60 miles a day. Whether this was a good idea or not is up for debate.

The positives of following this route were that it was largely very quiet, with little or no traffic, and it passed through many areas of stunning countryside and attractions. The negatives were that the journey was much longer (which I accepted), hillier, slower, and less comfortable (which I should have realised), and consequently perhaps more difficult than a more road-based LEJOG.

The traffic-free Sustrans routes and stunning countryside would be great for a leisurely day cycle, but not so much for getting from A to B with a time limit. The longer distance I could cope with that, but I discovered that some parts of the route made unnecessarily long detours, and some path surfaces left a lot to be desired.

People who would be drawn to this book, like me, wouldn't be keen road cyclists, serious amateurs or semi-professional, but would be leisurely cyclists looking for a safer route. So it's ironic that the route in the book is probably much more difficult than the route a fitter and stronger road cyclist would choose.

However, after saying all this, the question remains if I had done the cycle 'by the book'. i.e., over 4 weeks.

Would it have been more manageable? This is quite possible.

In any case, I mapped out an alternative route after returning home, cutting off corners and hillier sections, while still following potentially quiet roads and I managed to reduce dramatically the elevation and distance for the whole cycle.

Fitness & training.

I was a commuter cyclist and sat at an average level of fitness. So my training regime started with building on my commuting distance. My maximum commute was 14 miles, but more regularly I would commute 7 miles, so I started out doing 10 miles on my days off for a month and included some smaller hills. I started this in March for my LEJOG in August.

I ramped up the miles each month by 10 miles: April 20 miles, May 30 miles, June 40 miles, July 50 miles, and August 60 miles. I completed at least 4 cycles in a month and included hill routes up to 1200ft towards the end of my training.

On reflection, I could have done more hill training. Although little could have prepared me for some of the Cornish hills!

The bottom line however was that my cycles got easier and more enjoyable as the days progressed. I was getting fitter day after day. So I reckon if you can get over the first 3 or 4 days, then the rest is plain sailing. As mentioned earlier, it would be interesting to find out how difficult the Cornish hills were when cycling the other way, John O'Groats to Land's End.

Timings.

I planned my days in the app Komoot, setting the fitness slider to 'In Good Shape', which gave me the data I needed for how long the cycle would take each day. I tested out how accurate the Komoot times were on my training days, and 'In Good Shape' seemed to be about right.

This was a great guide but didn't quite work out on LEJOG.

In training, I was travelling roads and paths I already knew; I had either driven or cycled them before. Therefore I could zip along at a good pace and make the times that Komoot suggested.

On LEJOG a couple of factors affected these times.

I was on unfamiliar roads and had to slow down a little to pay more attention to where Komoot was directing me.

I used Komoot on an Android phone, set as a satnav, and to save battery power it was set to come on only when a turn was needed. The app wasn't very accurate in doing this so again I had to slow down to avoid missing turns and even then some were missed.

These factors probably added at least 10% to my journey times, and perhaps even more time through towns and cities.

To counteract this, on reflection, in planning taking the slider-setting down one notch in Komoot to 'Average' fitness would have given me more realistic times.

Komoot via the phone app was the most cost-effective way of navigation, but there are better ways to get cycle directions. You can still plan the route in Komoot, but if you then export it to a GPX file, this can be imported into a purpose-built navigation device, such as the Garmin Edge satnav.

Nutrition.

I didn't plan this well, which affected my performance & energy level on some days. To be honest I didn't plan my nutrition at all. I should have identified definite lunch and/or dinner stops along the way as I did with the campsites. It wouldn't have been too difficult to plan at least one proper meal a day – I failed miserably!

Also, I should have taken a camping stove and a lightweight pot or two. If nothing else I could have had a coffee each morning without having to trek for miles before I got my caffeine boost. Also on reflection, it would have saved me some weight, rather than adding to it. I could have purchased dried foods that just needed the addition of boiling water. Tins of beans and tuna pots, although convenient, just added to the weight I had to carry.

Accommodation

I was pleased with the accommodation along the way, and I think a proper bed at Manchester a third of the way, and at Cumbernauld two-thirds of the way, was a good plan.

I was surprised by how quickly and how well I took to camping, and by the time I had finished I was enjoying it so much I really didn't want to go back to a normal bed.

A consideration 'next time' would be to see if I could find Camping and Caravanning Club sites at suitable intervals. As I experienced at the Dingwall site, the club charges £8 a night for backpackers, which seems to include touring cyclists, and the sites seem to be very well run. As previously mentioned, however, you can't book the backpacker option on the website but have to phone the site itself to book.

Online tools

LEJOGers of the past had printed maps to guide their way, and in the past I had plotted car journeys in this way, stopping regularly when arriving at certain towns or landmarks to make sure I was on the right route. Checking road signs and road numbers and matching them to the map.

These days technology has opened up a whole new world, and although maps still have their place, online maps are now more common than the printed version. Not only that, but technology also allows maps to be interactive and guide us to our destination.

I used several map-based apps to plan and guide me on LEJOG. In the previous text, I described using Strava, Komoot, Polarsteps, Google Maps and Streetview, but these are only scratching the surface of the possibilities, and there are probably better tools out there. But these are the ones I used.

Certainly, on my return, these, and Google Maps Timeline, provided useful info for this book, by capturing my exact route, including all the wrong turns, recording all my timings, including start and finish times, plus lots of other data such as elevations and route profiles along the way.

Doing it solo.

My cycle was a self-imposed endurance test. I had no idea if I was going to complete LEJOG or fail. So with this in mind, I didn't want to take someone else, fail, and ruin their cycle too. The challenge was very personal, and like when I met Claire on the road, I didn't want anyone to slow down for, or try and keep up with.

For me, the instinct to make it from one end of the country to the other, under my own steam, being completely self-sufficient, was my personal goal. And the sense of achievement in completing this goal was indescribable.

Having said this, and now having successfully completed LEJOG, I think having others to cycle with 'next time' may be a good idea. Sharing each other's struggles, spurring each other on and supporting each other could make the journey less of a grind, and more enjoyable.

Alan Loach

So when are you going to do it?

There are of course lots of factors to take into account when thinking about cycling Land's End to John O'Groats. But age and fitness aren't necessarily barriers that can't be overcome. I would say the main factors are general health and determination.

A health condition at any age can appear to disqualify you, and you would be wise to seek professional medical advice before any attempt. But having said this, numerous people have faced challenges against the odds and have succeeded in attaining their goals.

It may not have been very apparent from the text of my journey, but I didn't push myself too hard most days, and I never broke a sweat, even on the days when I had to push a little harder. Each day was a slow-paced marathon rather than a fast sprint to the finish line.

I had the advantage of cycle commuting, which gave me a head start in training, but there's no reason why someone with little or no cycling experience couldn't build up enough strength and stamina over a longer period of time to attempt LEJOG.

The key is the determination to do it. It sounds easy on paper, but you need to be single-minded about getting out there and cycling, whatever the weather. Set a goal date of when you want to do the cycle. In simple terms, it's a case of working out a training plan that gradually increases over time and sticking to the plan.

Much of the training advice I've found on the Internet about cycling LEJOG is geared towards road bike, or racing bike, cyclists. But you don't need to be in as much of a hurry to finish as they do. At a slower pace and fewer miles per day, many people who can ride a bike could achieve LEJOG.

The NHS app 'Couch to 5k' is a good example of what someone can achieve by gradually building up the miles and stamina. There are also cycling apps where you can set goals and follow training plans, but most are subscription-based. Strava and Komoot are the ones that I use. I didn't personally set up any training plan through these apps but instead followed a simple regime of increasing my cycle mileage month by month until I was doing regular 60-mile cycles.

What I did do was set up local routes in Komoot, which allowed me to measure the distance of cycles and after the cycle was completed, measure my ongoing progress.

The approach is very much a personal thing and what worked for me may not work for you.

So the bottom line is, you might not be too old or too unfit to do LEJOG, so when are you going to do it?

Printed in Great Britain
by Amazon